VOLUME 31

Finland

J.E.O. Screen

Compiler

CLIO PRESS

OXFORD, ENGLAND · SANTA BARBARA, CALIFORNIA

British Library Cataloguing in Publication Data

Screen, J. E. O.
Finland. – (World bibliographical series; 31)
1. Finland – Bibliography
I. Title II. Series
016.948.97 Z5055

ISBN 0-903450-55-0

Clio Press Ltd.,
Woodside House, Hinksey Hill,
Oxford OX1 5BE, England.
Providing the services of the European Bibliographical Centre and the American Bibliographical Center.

American Bibliographical Center-Clio Press,
Riviera Campus, 2040 Alameda Padre Serra,
Santa Barbara, Ca. 93103, U.S.A.

Designed by Bernard Crossland
Computer typeset by Peter Peregrinus Ltd.
Printed in Great Britain

Finland

WORLD BIBLIOGRAPHICAL SERIES

General Editors:
Robert L. Collison (Editor-in-chief)
Sheila R. Herstein
Louis J. Reith
Hans H. Wellisch

OTHER VOLUMES IN THE SERIES

1 *Yugoslavia,* John J. Horton
2 *Lebanon,* Shereen Khairallah
3 *Lesotho,* Shelagh M. Willet and David Ambrose
4 *Rhodesia/Zimbabwe,* Oliver B. Pollack and Karen Pollack
5 *Saudi Arabia,* Frank A. Clements
6 *USSR,* Anthony Thompson
7 *South Africa,* Reuben Musiker
8 *Malawi,* Robert B. Boeder
9 *Guatemala,* Woodman B. Franklin
11 *Uganda,* Robert L. Collison
12 *Malaysia,* Lim Huck Tee and Wong Sook Jean
13 *France,* Frances Chambers
14 *Panama,* Eleanor Langstaff
15 *Hungary,* Thomas Kabdebo
16 *USA,* Sheila R. Herstein and Naomi Robbins
17 *Greece,* Richard Clogg and Mary Jo Clogg
18 *New Zealand,* R. F. Grover
19 *Algeria,* Richard Lawless
21 *Belize,* Ralph Lee Woodward, Jr
23 *Luxembourg,* Carlo Hury and Jul Christophory
24 *Swaziland,* Balam Nyeko
25 *Kenya,* Robert L. Collison
26 *India,* Brijen Gupta and Datta Kharbas
27 *Turkey,* Meral Güçlü
28 *Cyprus,* P. M. Kitromilides and M. Evriviades
29 *Oman,* Frank Clements
30 *Italy,* Emiliana P. Noether
32 *Poland,* Richard C. Lewanski

THE WORLD BIBLIOGRAPHICAL SERIES

This series will eventually cover every country in the world, each in a separate volume comprising annotated entries on works dealing with its history, geography, economy and politics; and with its people, their culture, customs, religion and social organization. Attention will also be paid to current living conditions – housing, education, newspapers, clothing etc. – that are all too often ignored in standard bibliographies; and to those particular aspects relevant to individual countries. Each volume seeks to achieve, by use of careful selectivity and critical assessment of the literature, an expression of the country and an appreciation of its nature and national aspirations, to guide the reader towards an understanding of its importance. The keynote of the series is to provide, in a uniform format, an interpretation of each country that will express its culture, its place in the world, and the qualities and background that make it unique.

SERIES EDITORS

Robert L. Collison (Editor-in-chief) is Professor Emeritus, Library and Information Studies, University of California, Los Angeles, and is currently the President of the Society of Indexers. Following the war, he served as Reference Librarian to the City of Westminster and later became Librarian to the BBC. During his fifty years as a professional librarian in England and the USA, he has written more than twenty works on bibliography, librarianship, indexing and related subjects.

Sheila R. Herstein is Reference Librarian and Library Instruction Coordinator at the City College of the City University of New York. She has extensive bibliographic experience and recently described her innovations in the field of bibliographic instruction in 'Team teaching and bibliographic instruction', *The Bookmark*, Autumn 1979. In addition, Professor Herstein co-authored a basic annotated bibliography in history for Funk & Wagnalls *New encyclopedia*, and for several years reviewed books for *Library Journal*.

Louis J. Reith is librarian with the Franciscan Institute, St. Bonaventure University, New York. He received his PhD from Stanford University, California, and later studied at Eberhard-Karls-Universität, Tübingen. In addition to his activities as a librarian, Dr. Reith is a specialist on 16th century German history and the Reformation, and has published many articles and papers in both German and English. He was also editor of the *American Society for Reformation Research Newsletter*.

Hans H. Wellisch is Associate Professor at the College of Library and Information Services, University of Maryland, and a member of the American Society of Indexers and the International Federation for Documentation. He is the author of numerous articles and several books on indexing and abstracting, and has most recently published *Indexing and abstracting: an international bibliography*. He also contributes frequently to *Journal of the American Society for Information Science, Library Quarterly*, and *The Indexer*.

Contents

Contents

Contents

Introduction

It is important for Finland to be both known and liked abroad. Although geographically remote – Finland is a very northern European state – the country has been drawn sufficiently often, and sufficiently recently, into major European conflicts to realize the dangers of isolation. As a small country that wants nothing better than to be left alone, Finland has nevertheless to come to terms with great power politics. The fact that the Soviet Union is Finland's eastern neighbour exerts a constant and powerful influence on the country. This influence is not without effect on the image of Finland abroad, notably in western Europe and North America. Finns frequently find it necessary to remind the uninformed Westerner that their country is neither a people's democracy nor a member of the Warsaw Pact; on the contrary, Finland is a Western style democracy, with a capitalist economy and, in spite of its security treaty with the USSR, a resolve to establish itself as a neutral state. There is a rarely expressed hope that if Finland succeeds in fostering this democratic and neutral image abroad its political, social and economic character may become less vulnerable to change through Soviet pressure. Every Finnish cultural event abroad, every international success by a Finnish athlete, every Finnish soldier contributed to a United Nations peace-keeping operation serves a useful purpose in a drive against isolation, in a determination to win friends abroad, and to gain the confidence of the great powers.

Finland is a sparsely populated country with some 4,745,000 inhabitants in an area rather more than twice the size of England and Wales. The pattern of settlement is strongly influenced by geography, with much of the population concentrated in the south and south-west, away from the Arctic north and the forested north-east. Finland's northern latitude gives it severe winters and short summers. Agriculture is not easy in such conditions and in the 19th century bad harvests were inexorably followed by famine. Finland, which had for many centuries an economy based on agriculture and forestry, now has an industrialized economy. The balance of population has shifted from the countryside to the towns. But many townsfolk retain rural roots and many industries are based on natural raw materials, particularly forest products. These are liable to feel quickly the effects of any recession in international trade and the economy is vulnerable, too, in that Finland has to import both oil and coal. Nevertheless, the standard of living is generally high and if there are few very rich Finns – by Western standards – there are few very poor.

The population is strikingly homogeneous. The Swedish-speaking minority numbers only about 6.5 per cent of the population and cannot be considered a race apart from the majority of Finnish speakers. The Lapps, who do constitute a separate group, number under 3,000 Lapp speakers. Language, which as late as the 1920s and 1930s was a divisive issue in society, is so no longer. The value of Swedish as a means of contact with the other northern countries is acknowledged by many Finnish speakers. The division between the rural and urban population finds some expression in politics but is less sharp than that between socialist and nonsocialist. Socialism in Finland was far from crushed by its defeat in the Civil War of 1918 that followed the declaration of independence; rather the extreme left has drawn inspiration and strength from that defeat. Finland's defeat by the USSR in 1944 was followed by the legalization of the Communist Party and that party, which with its allies attracts the support of some 20 per cent of the electorate, is now an established factor in political life, brought within the ordinary political process and drawn, on occasions, into government with other parties both socialist and nonsocialist.

Finnish governments have a reputation for short lives but, unlike the government coalitions, the presidency enjoys great stability. The president of the republic is no mere figurehead; he is a powerful director of affairs, with special responsibility in the field of foreign policy. Urho K. Kekkonen, who has been president since 1956, has vigorously pursued a policy of friendly relations with the Soviet Union against the background of the Treaty of Friendship, Cooperation and Mutual Assistance signed by the two countries – at Soviet instigation – in 1948. This treaty is directed to secure the USSR against an attack by Germany or any state allied with it and provides for Soviet help to Finland in the event of such an attack through Finnish territory. It provides too, for consultation between the two countries if an attack is threatened. Kekkonen's critics argue that he has gone further than he need in satisfying Soviet wishes both as regards Finnish internal policies and, for example, the pursuit of a nuclear free zone in northern Europe. Finland's eager support of détente may, however, be represented as a prudent desire to prevent the development of a crisis which could provoke consultation under the terms of the 1948 treaty that could be dangerous to Finland's independence. Nevertheless, the term 'Finlandization' has been coined, perhaps somewhat unfairly, to describe a country whose policy is subordinate to Soviet interests and which is being Sovietized without a revolutionary struggle.

Finland's internal freedom is obviously dependent on Soviet goodwill but Finnish political skill has undoubtedly played a part in its maintenance. That skill has contributed to the development of important connections with the West. Finnish trade with CMEA countries – notably the Soviet Union – does not amount to more than a quarter of Finland's foreign trade, and Finland has negotiated a significant trading agreement with the EEC, while it had previously an agreement with EFTA and older, close ties with the other Scandinavian countries through the Nordic Council. In its social policies and in its religious, legal and administrative traditions Finland has many affinities with its Scandinavian neighbours. Not for nothing was Finland a part of the kingdom of Sweden from the middle ages until 1809, when its incorporation into the Russian empire was accompanied by the creation and development of an autonomous government that was to facilitate the transition to independence after the Russian Revolution of 1917.

It was during the period of autonomy that the Finnish nation was truly formed, helped rather than hindered by the connection with Russia. Finnish literature dates from the 19th century though written Finnish goes back to the Reformation; Finnish art and architecture produced their own flourishing style at the end of the 19th century, and soon afterwards Finnish music attracted attention. In the arts, architecture and design Finland has exerted an influence abroad out of all proportion to its size. Finnish literature is less known in comparison but even so English translations of Finnish literature have achieved very considerable sales. The achievements of this small nation have aroused legitimate admiration and not only in cultural circles. The long tradition of Finnish success in Olympic athletics has won Finland wider acclaim, while the older generation remembers with respect the Finnish armed forces' heroic resistance to the Soviet invasion in the Winter War of 1939–40. Reserved but sincere, with an inner toughness – and in some cases an outer roughness – the Finns match well the characteristics of their rugged native land. And in a world that is not distinguished for its benevolent treatment of small nations the qualities of the Finns are their best guarantee of survival.

Introduction

The bibliography

Each volume in the World Bibliographical Series is intended to provide a selective, annotated bibliography covering all aspects of a particular country and is aimed 'at an audience ranging from the informed general reader to the scholar who wishes to obtain background information in a field other than his own'. Preference is given to recently published works and to material in English.

The compilation of this volume was completed in the late summer of 1980. The task of selection has not been easy since inevitably more material is to be found on some subjects than on others while it is impossible to find a representative selection of Finnish literature in translation. However, it is hoped that the resulting book will meet at least some of the needs of those seeking sources of information about Finland. Where nothing is found on a particular topic, the reader is advised to turn to the introductory works in the first chapter. It should be noted that the chapter on periodicals includes only periodicals of a general character and newspapers; references to other periodicals will be found in the appropriate chapters. Present publishers are given for serial publications. Although Finland is a country of two official languages, Finnish and Swedish, little information has been provided about the Swedish language since the reader is more likely to look for it in another volume of the series. The publisher is responsible for the solecism that places of publication of Swedish-language works appear in their Finnish-language forms.

Readers wishing to buy Finnish books will frequently find the use of a bookseller in Finland swifter and cheaper than ordering through a local bookseller. Two large Finnish bookshops supplying customers abroad are: Akateeminen Kirjakauppa, Keskuskatu 1, 00100 Helsinki 10, and Suomalainen Kirjakauppa, Aleksanterinkatu 23, 00100 Helsinki 10. The postal address of the Finnish Government Printing Centre, which supplies government publications, is: Valtion Painatuskeskus, PL 516, 00101 Helsinki 10. The inter-library loan system should, of course, be able to help in obtaining material listed in the bibliography.

Acknowledgements

Many friends and colleagues in Britain and Finland have assisted me with suggestions and comments during the preparation of this bibliography. Without their help the task would have been much harder, and I am most grateful to them. Especial thanks are due to the Information

Centre for Finnish Literature (Secretary, Miss Marja-Leena Rautalin) for a grant to enable me to visit Finland in March 1979, to Professor Esko Häkli, Chief Librarian of Helsinki University Library, for assisting with my programme and in other ways, and to the School of Slavonic and East European Studies, University of London, for a brief period of leave of absence.

Introductory Works

Finland in general works on Scandinavia

1 **Scandinavia.**
W. R. Mead, Wendy Hall. London: Thames & Hudson, 1972. 208p. map. bibliog.

This is a well-balanced survey covering the geographical and historical background and 'the Scandinavian contribution' in social policy, design and Nordic integration. It considers the Scandinavian countries together rather than separately, though p. 80-94 are devoted specifically to Finland.

2 **Scandinavia.**
Franklin D. Scott. Cambridge, Massachusetts; London: Harvard University Press, 1975. [xi]+330p. map. bibliog. (The American Foreign Policy Library).

A revised and enlarged edition of *The United States and Scandinavia*. A good introductory book, written from an American viewpoint.

3 **The Scandinavians.**
Donald S. Connery. London: Eyre & Spottiswoode; New York: Simon & Schuster, 1966. xvi+590p. map. bibliog.

Part One (p. 1-80) gives an impression of Scandinavia and Part Five (p. 441-547) of Finland. Connery's shrewd observations are still worth reading.

Older descriptions

4 **Travels through Sweden, Finland, and Lapland, to the North Cape in the years 1798 and 1799.**

Joseph Acerbi. London: printed for Joseph Mawman, 1802. 2 vols. map.

Giuseppe Acerbi (1773-1846) was born near Mantua. His *Travels* describes the journey in Scandinavia which he undertook with the son of a rich banker from Brescia. Crossing from Stockholm to Turku via the Åland Islands, he continued to Vaasa, Oulu and Kemi and into Lapland. His account and observations are very readable and remain full of interest, particularly the material on Lapland.

5 **Travels in various countries of Europe, Asia and Africa. Part the third: Scandinavia.**

Edward Daniel Clarke. London: Cadell & Davies, 1819-23. 2 vols. maps.

Edward Daniel Clarke (1769-1822), a Cambridge mineralogist, was a notable traveller who visited Scandinavia in 1799-1800. 'Section the first' includes Lapland and Ostrobothnia; 'Section the second' is mainly concerned with a journey from Stockholm to St. Petersburg via the Åland Islands, Turku, Helsinki and Viipuri. Clarke did not travel without experiencing danger. His style is attractive, his observations careful and still significant.

6 **Finland in the nineteenth century.**

Helsinki: Tilgmann, 1894. 367+IXp. maps.

An extensive and richly illustrated survey of Finland at the end of the 19th century, which pays attention to scholarship and literature as well as to the country, the people and politics. It reflects throughout the aspirations of the emergent Finnish nation.

7 **Through Finland in carts.**

Mrs. Alec Tweedie. London: Black, 1897. [xii]+366p. map.

This lively account by an intrepid and perceptive lady traveller was a great commercial success (it was frequently reprinted) and it remains entertaining.

8 **Letters from Finland, August, 1908-March, 1909.**

Rosalind Travers. London: Kegan Paul, Trench, Trübner, 1911. xi+404p. map.

The author's exceptional knowledge of Finland and Finnish politics make this book still worth reading as more than a travel account.

9 **Finland: the country, its people and institutions.**

Helsinki: Otava, 1926. 598+[i]+viip. maps.

This large work by various eminent Finns covers all aspects of the country and of Finnish life and culture. As an account of the newly independent state, and as an expression of its self-confidence, the book retains considerable value.

10 **Finland.**

J. Hampden Jackson. London: Allen & Unwin, 1940. 2nd rev. ed. 243p. maps.

Originally published in 1938, the book was revised to take account of the Russian invasion up to the beginning of 1940. Half history, half a description of the new republic, Jackson's work remains interesting as an intelligent period piece.

Recent descriptions

11 **Finland.**

W. R. Mead. London: Benn, 1968. 256p. maps. bibliog.

The best of the recent background books, containing a sound geographical base, a good deal of history, and enough economics and culture to give the reader a lively picture of the modern nation and how it has developed. The author is Professor of Geography at University College, London, and the doyen of British scholars concerned with Finland. The book has a discursive bibliographical appendix.

12 **The identity of Finland.**

W. R. Mead. *Contemporary Review*, vol. 235, no. 1363 (Aug. 1979), p. 57-62.

Contrasts the stereotyped international image of Finland with the realities of material progress and artistic resurgence. A very good, brief introductory essay, which comments - significantly - on Finland's new-found Scandinavian affluence and its growing maturity.

13 **Finland: an introduction.**

Edited by Sylvie Nickels, Hillar Kallas, Philippa Friedman. London: Allen & Unwin, 1973. 377p. map. bibliog.

A good introductory work by authoritative contributors, covering many aspects of Finnish history, politics, geography, trade and culture. Includes a useful bibliography of books in English about Finland. The book is an extensive revision of *Finland: creation and construction* edited by Hillar Kallas and Sylvie Nickels (London: Allen & Unwin; New York: Praeger; Helsinki: Werner Söderström, 1968. 366p. map. bibliog).

14 **Area handbook for Finland. Prepared for the American University by the Institute for Cross-Cultural Research.**

Theodore L. Stoddard. Washington, DC: US Government Printing Office, 1974. xiv+259p. maps. bibliog.

'One of a series of handbooks prepared under the auspices of Foreign Area Studies of the American University, designed to be useful to military and other personnel who need a convenient compilation of basic facts about...various countries.' Separate sections entitled Social, Political, Economic, and National Security. A very good basic survey with an excellent bibliography, mostly of material in English, and a useful index.

15 **Finland, 1918-1968: a lecture delivered 5 December 1968.**
Heikki Waris. London: University College, 1970. 31p. maps. (Scandinavian Studies Jubilee Lectures).

Summarizes the characteristics of Finland as a borderland, a Scandinavian land, and a homogeneous society; describes briefly its political development, economic growth and social change, and standard of living during the period of independence. A very good overview by a leading social scientist, with maps and figures to support the text.

16 **Facts about Finland.**
Helsinki: Otava, 1979. 16th rev. ed. 109p. maps. bibliog.

A regularly updated little volume which packs in a great deal of useful basic information about the land and the people, history, the state, the economy, social welfare, schools and education, sport and travel.

17 **Finland: facts and figures.**
Edited by Jyrki Leskinen. Helsinki: Otava, 1979. 2nd rev. ed. 239p. maps. bibliog.

Similar in structure to *Facts about Finland* (q.v.) but larger and more discursive. Supplementary information includes 'Useful addresses of organisations in Finland' (in classified order), a short bibliography of works in English, and statistics.

18 **Introduction to Finland 1960.**
Edited by Urho Toivola. Porvoo, Finland: Werner Söderström, 1960. 313p. map. bibliog.

19 **Introduction to Finland 1963.**
Edited by Göran Stenius. Porvoo, Finland: Werner Söderström, 1963. 291p. map. bibliog.

There is little duplication between this volume and the preceding one, although both are collections of articles rather than comprehensive surveys. Between them, they contain much complementary information about history, geography, politics, the economy, education, culture, sport and religion. Most of the articles are by Finnish authorities but a few are by foreign experts. Both books are indexed in the 1963 volume; that for 1960 has its own index.

20 **Finland 1917-1967: an assessment of independence.**
Helsinki: Kirjayhtymä, 1967. 172p.

A mixed bag of seven articles by prominent Finns, touching on history, the constitution and security policy in the period 1917-67. Following these are nearly 100 pages of well-chosen black-and-white photographs depicting significant events and personalities as well as scenes of ordinary life from 1900 to the time of publication.

21 **The Finns and their country.**
Wendy Hall. London: Parrish, 1967. 224p. map. bibliog.
A readable and sympathetic introductory sketch of Finland, which is a continuation and revision of the author's *Green gold and granite: a background to Finland* (London: Parrish, 1957. 2nd rev. ed. 190p. map. bibliog.).

22 **The Finns and the Lapps: how they live and work.**
John L. Irwin. Newton Abbot, England: David & Charles, 1973. reprinted, 1978. 171p. maps.
Chapters include: How the country is run; How they live; How they work; How they learn; How they get about; How they amuse themselves. Two chapters are devoted to the Lapps. Informative, but much of the detailed information has dated rapidly. Though reprinted, not revised.

23 **Finland.**
Gladys Nicol. London: Batsford, 1975. 216p. map.
A combination of travel book and background book: still useful for the intending visitor.

24 **Finland.**
Walter Bacon. London: Hale, 1970. 304p. maps. bibliog.
An introductory book with geographical and rather more historical information together with sections on life in present-day Finland. The latter sections are informative without giving excessive and easily dated detail.

25 **The land and people of Finland.**
Erick Berry. Philadelphia; New York: Lippincott, 1972. rev. ed. 160p. map. (Portrait of a Nation Series).
An American writer's introduction to Finland, set largely in a historical framework. Some interesting impressions as well as some misleading ones.

Finland in the twentieth century.
See item no. 122.

Finland: a Scandinavian modern country.
See item no. 234.

Picture books

26 **Finlandia: kuvia Suomesta. Pictures of Finland.**
Text by Kalervo Siikala. Helsinki: Kirjahytmä, 1979. 2nd ed. [136]p. map.
Varied coloured illustrations accompanied by a good text.

27 **Days in Finland.**
Osmo Thiel, Matti Käki. Helsinki: Otava, 1972. [i.e. 1974]. 5th printing. [128]p.

A very good picture book indeed, with excellent colour photographs of the Finnish landscape, towns, people, industry, etc., and a short, sensible introduction by Matti Käki.

28 **Finlandia: profile of a country.**
Mario De Biasi, Göran Stenius. London: Evelyn, 1967. 156p. map.

A very pleasing selection of photographs (some in colour) by De Biasi and a sensitive text by the writer Göran Stenius, with many well-chosen quotations.

29 **Meet the Finns.**
Mario De Biasi, Erkki Savolainen. Helsinki: Tammi, 1969. 32+[96]p.

The photographs by De Biasi - some in colour - are above average in quality and variety of subject. The introduction by Erkki Savolainen presents a cheerful characterization of Finland.

30 **Suomalainen järvi. Finland: sjöarnas land. Finnland: ein Land der Seen. Finland: a land of lakes.**
Matti A. Pitkänen, Jaakko Napola. Espoo, Finland: Weilin & Göös, 1978. 162p. maps.

Fine photographs of Finland's notable lake scenery by Matti A. Pitkänen, the country's most famous landscape photographer. Text by Jaakko Napola in Finnish, Swedish, German and English.

31 **Suomalainen maisema. Die Finnische Landschaft. The Finnish landscape. Det finländska landskapet.**
Matti A. Pitkänen, Teuvo Suominen. Helsinki: Weilin & Göös, 1974. 2nd ed. 188p.

Photographs by Matti A. Pitkänen and text by Teuvo Suominen in Finnish, Swedish, German and English. The colour and black-and-white photographs are of excellent quality but somewhat didactic in purpose - a concluding section, 'Man', shows damage to the environment.

32 **Suomalaisia kuvia. Finland i bild. Finnland in Bildern. Finland in pictures.**
Matti A. Pitkänen, Raimo Kojo. Helsinki: Weilin & Göös, 1978. 3rd ed. 336p.

Short introduction by Raimo Kojo and picture captions in Finnish, Swedish, German and English. Magnificent photographs (colour and black-and-white) by Matti A. Pitkänen, arranged geographically and composed to show the natural features of Finland though also covering places and sights of cultural and historical importance, folk ceremonies and events. Not a complete picture of Finland but a very beautiful one.

33 **Finland: land of the midnight sun. Finnland: Land der Mitternachtssonne.**
Helsinki: Reader's Digest, 1978. 280p. maps.
Compiled to show the beauty of Finland and does so very successfully; informative text in English and German.

34 **The landscape of Finland.**
Renaud Rosset, Patrick Degommier. Helsinki: Otava, 1974. 64p.
Agreeable photographs by Patrick Degommier; the text by Renaud Rosset might best be characterized as evocative.

35 **Noin sata Suomeni maisemaa: kaksisataa valokuvaa ja yksi kartta Suomestani vuosilta 1973-1977. My Finland: two hundred pictures.** (About a hundred landscapes of my Finland: two hundred photographs and one map of my Finland from the years 1973-77.)
Markku Tanttu. Helsinki: Markku Tanttu, 1978. 112p. map.
A very personal collection of black-and-white photographs, possessing considerable charm and interest.

Books for children

36 **How people live in Finland.**
W. R. Mead. London: Ward Lock Educational, 1965. 112p. maps. bibliog.
This simply written and highly informative description of the life of various Finns in different parts of the country distils the author's knowledge and understanding of Finland and its geography. Intended for young readers, it can be read with profit by specialists.

37 **My home in Finland.**
Susan Howard. London: Longman, 1962. reprinted, 1969. 17p.
One of a series of tiny books for children about how children live in various countries. Gives a good, if a little old-fashioned, impression of Finnish life, helped by interesting illustrations.

38 **Matti lives in Finland.**
Astrid Lindgren, Anna Riwkin-Brick. London: Methuen, 1969. [48]p. (Children Everywhere Series).
A pleasant story for children by Astrid Lindgren about a Finnish country boy, illustrated with excellent photographs by Anna Riwkin-Brick.

39 **Finland in pictures.**
David A. Boehm. New York: Sterling; London: Oak Tree Press, 1977. 13th printing. 64p. map. (Visual Geography Series).

Originally published in 1963, this book for older children appears dated in its illustrations but the text has been at least partially revised.

40 **Let's visit Finland.**
Alan James. London; Norwalk, Connecticut; Ajax, Canada: Burke, 1979. 96p. map. (Let's Visit...).

This nicely illustrated book, which conveys a fairly accurate impression of modern Finland, will appeal to older children.

41 **The young traveller in Finland.**
Sylvie Nickels. London: Phoenix House, 1962. 127p. map.

Describes the adventures in Finland of two English children who travel there with their father and two young Finnish friends. Within the framework of the fictional journey, the book imparts a lot of information about Finland and its people, at the price of some heavy dialogue.

42 **Finland: champion of independence.**
Leonora Curtin Paloheimo, Jane Werner Watson. Champaign, Illinois: Garrard, 1969. 112p. maps.

Facts are interspersed with stories to give children an impression of the state of Finland and the condition of life there.

Geography

Maps and atlases

43 **Maanteiden yleiskartta. Översiktskarta över landsvägarna. Suomi - Finland. General road map of Finland. Landstrassen Übersichtskarte über Finnland.**
Helsinki: Maanmittaushallitus, 1980. 1 sheet.

A general road map of Finland at a scale of 1:1,500,000, published annually by the Map Service of the National Board of Survey (P.O. Box 209, 00131 Helsinki 13), which also issues an English language 'price-list of maps' setting out the different types and scales of maps available.

44 **Autoilijan tiekartta. Bilistens vägkarta. Motoring road map. Auto Strassenkarte. Suomi ja Pohjoiskalotti. Finland och Nordkalotten. Finland and the North Calotte. Finnland und die Nordkalotte.**
Helsinki: Maanmittaushallitus, 1980. 2 sheets. annual.

Covers Finland and the north of Sweden and Norway (the North Calotte) at a scale of 1:800,000.

45 **Suomen tiekartta. Vägkarta över Finland. Road map of Finland. Finnische Strassenkarte.**
Helsinki: Maanmittaushallitus, 1976-80. 19 sheets.

Gives topographical as well as road information. The scale is 1:200,000. For indexes of place-names listed in this and the preceding item, see *Suomi. Finland. Uusi yleiskarttakirja. Nya generalkartboken* (q.v.).

46 **Suomi. Finland. Uusi yleiskarttakirja. Nya generalkartboken.** (New general atlas.)
Helsinki: Maanmittaushallitus, 1977. 93p. maps.

As well as topographical maps of the whole country at a scale of 1:400,000, this atlas published by the National Board of Survey includes sections on soil, water, peatlands, forests, nature protection, rural settlement and seasons. It also shows (on p. 62) the state of map coverage of Finland at 30 April 1977 in respect of the basic map (1:20,000) and the topographic maps (1:20,000 and 1:100,000). There is an index of place-names which can also be used with the motoring road map (1:800,000) (no. 44) and the road map of Finland (1:200,000) (no. 45). Directions for use appear in English as well as Finnish, Swedish and German.

47 **Fennia. Suuri Suomi-kartasto. Kartverk över Finland. Finland in maps. Finnischer Atlas.**
Helsinki: Weilin & Göös, 1979. 224p. maps.

At 1:250,000 this is the largest-scale atlas published of Finland. The fine maps are published by the National Board of Survey. The atlas also includes a gazetteer of 9,000 places, town plans, and information about the availability of maps at other scales.

48 **Atlas de Finlande.** (Atlas of Finland.)
Helsinki: Société de Géographie de Finlande, 1899. 2 vols. maps.

This is the first of an excellent series of national atlases published by the Geographical Society of Finland, of which the older volumes retain considerable value since they measure the changing circumstances of Finland, both physical and human. The maps include climate, vegetation, population, schools, agriculture, industry, transport and communications, prehistoric finds, historic frontiers, and reproductions of the maps of Olaus Magnus (1539) and Andreas Bureus (1626). The introductory material to the atlas volume includes statistics of area and population by administrative division. The atlas was published in two editions, one in French, the other in Finnish and Swedish. The text volume, published separately in Finnish, Swedish and French (the last being in the series *Fennia* [q.v.], vol. 17), gives full comments and explanations of the maps individually.

49 **Atlas de Finlande. 1910.** (Atlas of Finland. 1910.)
Helsinki: Société Géographique de Finlande, 1911. 3 vols. maps.

This is a greatly expanded version of the 1899 atlas. The atlas itself was published in a single edition, with captions in Finnish, Swedish and French; the text was published separately in each language, the last as *Fennia*, vol. 30. Volume 1 of the text provides a detailed explanation of twenty-three maps covering the land, water, meteorology, flora, vegetation, fauna and forests of Finland, while volume 2 explains twenty-seven maps covering population, agriculture, industry, languages, education, towns, etc.

50 **Suomen kartasto. Atlas of Finland. Atlas över Finland. 1925.**
Geographical Society of Finland. Helsinki: Otava, 1925-29. 2 vols. maps.

Detailed explanation of the maps on the same lines as the 1910 atlas but with additional coverage of mining, industry, foreign trade, shipping, banking, cooperation, postal services, education, health, boundaries, etc. The atlas was published in a single edition, with its captions in Finnish, Swedish and English; the text appeared in separate editions in each of those languages, the English appearing as *Fennia*, vol. 48.

51 **Suomen kartasto. Atlas of Finland. Atlas över Finland. 1960.**
Geographical Society of Finland and University of Helsinki Department of Geography. Helsinki: Otava, 1960-62. 2 vols. maps.

Follows a similar pattern of coverage to the 1925 atlas but with less detailed notes.

52 **Suomen kartasto. Atlas över Finland. Atlas of Finland.**
Helsinki: National Board of Survey and Geographical Society of Finland, 1976- . maps.

Two fascicles have appeared so far of this new edition of the *Atlas of Finland*, which was scheduled for completion in 1985. Folio 234, Forestry, was published in 1976, and folio 311, Public Administration, in 1977. Maps and figures appear in Finnish, Swedish and English. The accompanying articles are in Finnish but Swedish and English translations are available as enclosures.

53 **Atlas över Skärgårds-Finland. Saaristo-Suomen kartasto. Atlas of the archipelago of southwestern Finland.**
Helsinki: Nordenskiöld-Samfundet i Finland, 1960. 2 vols. maps.

Published by the Nordenskiöld Society of Finland, this is a very detailed study of a comparatively small but characteristic region of Finland. The atlas is in two parts: 1, General features: natural history, human geography and history; 2, Typical villages: natural vegetation, crops, land tenure and settlement. The captions to the maps are in Swedish, Finnish and English, but the detailed explanations in volume 2 (the text to the atlas) are in Swedish only.

54 **Vanhoja Suomen karttoja. Old maps of Finland.**
Isak Gordin. Helsinki: Kustannuskilta, 1973. 2nd rev. ed. 111p. maps.

A handsome volume which comprises forty-seven pages of reproductions of printed maps and charts showing Finland and dating from between 1482 and 1799. The brief annotations and introduction are in Finnish and English. The book gives an excellent impression of the development of the cartographers' image of Finland.

55 **Suomen historian kartasto. Atlas of Finnish history.**
Edited by Eino Jutikkala. Porvoo, Finland: Werner Söderström, 1959. 2nd rev. ed. 83p. maps. (Suomen tiedettä [Finnish Science], 2).

Introduction and captions in Finnish and English. Includes maps on population and settlement, ecclesiastical and civil administrative divisions, campaigns, farming, industry, trade, towns, communications and schools.

56 **Scandinavian atlas of historic towns.**
[Odense, Denmark]: Danish Committee for Urban History; Odense University Press, 1977. Vols. 1-2.

Volume 1: *Finland: Turku-Åbo* by Eino Jutikkala. 10p. maps; volume 2: *Finland Borgå-Porvoo* by Eino Jutikkala, 11p. maps. These first two fascicles, of an atlas intended to comprise fifteen, are devoted to Finland. For Turku there is a reproduction of a coloured map (1:5,000) showing the town in 1741-43 and a reproduction of a plan on the same scale for 1808 on which occupations have been plotted. For Porvoo there is a reproduction of a coloured map (1:2,500) from 1792, a plan on the same scale showing occupations in 1694-96, and another showing buildings in the 1830s. The texts include maps showing the towns in their localities, and describe the history and development of the towns as well as describing the maps themselves. The text of the atlas is in English, Finnish and Swedish.

Glossaries and gazetteers

57 **Short glossary of Finnish.**
London: Geographical Section General Staff, War Office, 1943. 11p.

A glossary of over 500 Finnish terms likely to be encountered on maps, with translations into English and, where appropriate, the abbreviations for the terms in Finnish.

58 **A glossary of Finnish map terms and abbreviations.**
A. E. Palmerlee. Cleveland, Ohio: Micro Photo Division, Bell & Howell Company, 1968. [iv]+iii+50p.

An expansion of a glossary originally compiled in 1959. Covers geological as well as topographical and administrative terms. Also has some Lapp words (designated as such), and some archaisms. Comprises some 1,200 terms and abbreviations.

59 **Finland. Official standard names approved by the United States Board on Geographic Names.**
Washington, DC: US Government Printing Office, 1962. vi+556p. map. (Gazetteer No. 62).

About 39,800 entries for places and features in Finland, the map scale of the name coverage being approximately 1:400,000. There is a glossary of generic terms.

Fennia. Suuri Suomi-kartasto. Kartverk över Finland. Finland in maps. Finnischer Atlas.
See item no. 47.

Finland as a part of Scandinavia

60 **Scandinavia.**

Brian Fullerton, Alan F. Williams. London: Chatto & Windus, 1975. 2nd ed. xiv+375p. maps. bibliog.

'Intended as an introduction to the geography of Scandinavia for students, business men and prospective travellers.' Covers Denmark, Finland, Norway and Sweden, with common introductory material, and a concluding chapter on international trade and relations. Chapters 19-22 deal with Finland; first an 'economic introduction', then southern Finland, the Finnish lake plateau, and northern Finland. Each chapter has a reading list and there is a bibliography.

61 **A geography of Norden: Denmark, Finland, Iceland, Norway, Sweden.**

Edited by Axel Sømme. London: Heinemann, 1968. new ed. [354+45]p. maps. bibliog.

An extensive, scholarly standard work by a number of Scandinavian geographers, the late Professor Helmer Smeds contributing the chapter on Finland (p. 155-203). Physical geography is treated mainly in the general chapters, while the individual country chapters concentrate on human and economic geography.

62 **An advanced geography of northern and western Europe.**

R. J. Harrison Church, Peter Hall, G. R. P. Lawrence, W. R. Mead, Alice F. A. Mutton. Amersham, England: Hulton Educational Publications, 1980. 3rd ed. 480p. maps. bibliog.

Chapter 4: Finland (p. 53-71) is by Professor Mead and provides a very good survey of the geography of the country. Written for sixth-form students.

63 **An economic geography of the Scandinavian states and Finland.**

W. R. Mead. London: University of London Press, 1958. [xvi]+302p. maps.

Discusses the economic geography of the region within the framework of the twin variables of natural resources and the human element. Examines particularly farming, fisheries, sources of energy, the network of communications, the softwood industries and mining and metallurgy.

64 **The Scandinavian northlands.**

W. R. Mead. London: Oxford University Press, 1974. 48p. maps. bibliog. (Problem Regions of Europe).

Looks at the barren areas of northern Finland, Sweden and Norway, which have become known as Nordkalotten (the North Calotte), and at their problems, both economic and political, and possible solutions to them. Written for sixth-form students.

General geography

65 **Suomi: a general handbook on the geography of Finland.**
Helsinki: Geographical Society of Finland, 1952. x+626p. maps. (*Fennia*, 72).

A dated but very thorough presentation by authorities in various fields: 'the main stress has been placed on presenting Finland as a physical and cultural geographic unit, without focussing attention on smaller regions and their interaction'.

66 **Finland and its geography: an American Geographical Society handbook.**
Edited by Raye R. Platt. New York: Duell, Sloan & Pearce, 1955. xxv+510p. maps. bibliog.

Designed for 'the general intelligent reading public', this is an extensive work about government, population, disease geography, agriculture, industries, the cooperative movement, transport and commerce, as well as cartography, climate, vegetation, the geographical regions and geology. The main sources (many in English) are listed at the end of each chapter. Some of the information is, of course, now out of date but very much remains in the book that is still worthwhile.

67 **Fennia.**
Helsinki: Geographical Society of Finland, 1889- .

A series comprising monograph-length works on the geography of Finland in all its aspects, and now written in English. Two or three issues a year.

68 **Terra. Suomen Maantieteellisen Seuran aikakauskirja. Geografiska sällskapets i Finland tidskrift. Journal of the Geographical Society of Finland.**
Helsinki: Suomen Maantieteellinen Seura, 1889- . quarterly.

Originally published as *Geografiska föreningens tidskrift. Maantieteellisen yhdistyksen aikakauskirja* (Journal of the Geographical Society of Finland), 1889-1912, vols. 1-24, *Terra* now publishes articles not simply - though most frequently - on Finland, with abstracts or summaries in English, and reviews.

Special aspects

69 **Recent developments in human geography in Finland.**
W. R. Mead. *Progress in Human Geography*, vol. 1, no. 3 (1977), p. 361-75. bibliog.

'This short review of developments in human geography in Finland outlines the institutional framework within which the subject is pursued, identifies the principal areas of research, recalls the tradition of mapmaking, casts an eye over the contributions from cognate disciplines and the process of reappraisal and concludes with a comment on geography in the sixty-year old Finnish state.' There is (on p. 372-75) a bibliography of significant contributions to the subject during the previous twenty-five years.

70 **Winter in Finland.**
W. R. Mead, Helmer Smeds. London: Evelyn; New York: Praeger, 1967. 144p. maps. bibliog.

Winter exerts a profound influence on all aspects of life and work in Finland. This book is a scholarly consideration of the problems posed by winter in Finland and the solutions adopted to deal with them.

71 **Finland: daughter of the sea.**
Michael Jones. Folkestone, England: Dawson; Hamden, Connecticut: Archon, 1977. 247p. maps. (Studies in Historical Geography).

'Land emergence is one of the most fascinating physical phenomena of Finland' (Mead). Jones's study describes land uplift in Finland in its physical, human and legal respects.

72 **The Åland Islands.**
W. R. Mead, S. H. Jaatinen. Newton Abbot, England: David & Charles, 1975. 183p. maps. bibliog.

Describes the geography and history of the Åland Islands, paying particular attention to the development of society and the economy, and to the problems confronting these 'fortunate islands' today.

73 **Saltvik: studies from an Åland parish.**
W. R. Mead, and members of the Geographical Field Group. Nottingham, England: Geographical Field Group, 1964. [i]+63p. maps. (Geographical Field Group Regional Studies, 10).

An assembly of studies - on land form, soil, population and farming - made by a party of British geographers in Saltvik in 1963. Contains much detail on Åland not available elsewhere.

Environment

74 **The fight to save our wildlife.**
Teuvo Suominen. *Look at Finland*, no. 1 (1973), p. 10-19.

An illustrated, popular account of the state of conservation of Finnish birds and animals.

75 **Symposium on man's influence on nature in Finland.**
Edited by Ilmari Hustich. *Fennia*, vol. 85 (1961), 128p. maps. bibliog.

Papers, summaries of papers, and discussions (in English, Swedish, German and Finnish) from a symposium arranged in 1959 by the Geographical Society of Finland, the Zoological and Botanical Society Vanamo and the Societas pro Fauna et Flora Fennica. Apart from a general historical survey, topics dealt with included water supply and the influence of man on various types of flora and fauna.

76 **Man and the Baltic Sea.**
Helsinki: Finnish Baltic Sea Committee, Ministry of the Interior, 1977. 34p. maps.

The Convention on the Protection of the Marine Environment of the Baltic Sea Area was signed in Helsinki by all the Baltic Sea States in 1974. It attempts to reduce pollution in the Baltic. This booklet sets out the history of the Baltic Sea, its importance, and the growth of pollution that lay behind the conclusion of the convention.

77 **The principles of water pollution control up to 1985.**
Helsinki: National Board of Waters, 1974. 40p. maps. (Publications of the National Board of Waters, 12).

Describes measures to reduce the waste water load on watercourses and to halt 'creeping pollution'. The maps illustrate the effects of the proposed measures.

78 **Town and country planning law in Finland.**
Tore Modeen. In: *Planning law in western Europe*. Edited by J. F. Garner. Amsterdam; Oxford, England; North-Holland; New York: American Elsevier, 1975, p. 101-15. bibliog.

One of a number of studies of the law relating to land use planning or town and country planning in various countries. This chapter surveys the historical, constitutional and legal background to Finnish planning law, examines the provisions of the Planning and Building Act of 1958 and subsequent legislation, and describes the types of plan that can be made and the controls that exist over planning.

79 **Physical planning in Finland.**
Helsinki: Ministry of the Interior, 1975. 50p.

Describes the administration involved in planning and building, reviews legislation on land use, and provides some detail on land use planning and physical planning.

80 **Developing local planning in Finland.**
Heikki Koski. *Planning and Administration*, vol. 4, no. 2 (autumn 1977), p. 39-48.

'Focuses on efforts aimed at qualitative improvement' in local planning 'by increasing the opportunity and the desire of citizens to take an active part in the planning process'.

Tourism and travel

81 **Finland handbook: 1980.**
Helsinki: Finnish Tourist Board, 1980. 168p. map. bibliog.

A annual produced for the travel trade by the Finnish Tourist Board and the leading tourist organizations in Finland. Gives information about coming events, entry formalities, facts about Finnish tourist regions and towns, air and sea connections to Finland, transportation within the country, tours, leisure time activities, types of accommodation, etc.

82 **Finland 80: welcome to Finland. Soyez les bienvenus en Finlande. Willkommen in Finnland.**
Zug, Switzerland: Anders Nyborg, 1980. 19th ed. 202p.

A glossy, trilingual annual, supported by extensive advertising. Each issue contains a number of well-illustrated background articles.

83 **[Pamphlets].**
Helsinki: Finnish Tourist Board.

The Finnish Tourist Board publishes a number of pamphlets each year which provide essential and accurate information on their subjects. *Camping* lists camping sites and youth hostels; *Hotels* lists hotels by locality; *Motoring routes* gives general information for motorists as well as eight tour routes; *Timetables and fares* provides advance information about transport services; *Travel facts* is a brief compendium about travel, accommodation, etc. Pamphlets and information may be obtained from the Finnish Tourist Board UK Office, 66 Haymarket, London SW1Y 4RF, or in the United States from the Finnish National Tourist Office, 75 Rockefeller Plaza, New York, NY 10019.

84 **Suomen hotelliopas 1980. Hotelguide Finland.**
Helsinki: Suomen Matkailuliitto, 1980. 55th ed. 106p. maps.

The Finnish Travel Association first published this guide in 1926. The 1980 edition contains information in Finnish, Swedish, English and German about 758 establishments - hotels, motels and inns.

85 **Leirintäalueopas 1980. Camping in Finland.**
Helsinki: Suomen Matkailuliitto, 1980. 352p. maps.

An annual publication providing details of camping sites. Includes an explanation of symbols and a very brief introduction in English.

86 **Wonderland for canoeing.**
Anja Smolander. *Look at Finland*, no. 2 (1979), p. 30-33.

A practical guide on where and how to canoe in Finland, with a section on how to obtain further information.

Suomen kulkuneuvot. Finlands kommunikationer. (Finnish Transport.)
See item no. 387.

Look at Finland.
See item no. 734.

Historical guidebooks

87 **Handbook for northern Europe, including Denmark, Norway, Sweden, Finland and Russia. Part I: Denmark, Norway and Sweden. Part II: Finland and Russia.**

John Murray. London: John Murray, 1848-49. new ed. 2 vols. maps. Part II, section IV: Finland, p. 349-78.

A fascinating guide for travellers in the pre-railway age. 'Nervous people have no business to travel in Finland', although 'the living in Finland we found very tolerable'.

88 **Russia with Teheran, Port Arthur, and Peking: handbook for travellers.**

Karl Baedeker. Leipzig, GDR: Baedeker, 1914. lxiv+590p. maps. Reprinted, London: Allen & Unwin; Newton Abbot, England: David & Charles, 1971. [ii] + lxiv + 590p. maps.

Part IV: The Grand Duchy of Finland, p. 197-246, provides a mine of information on Finland as it was at the end of the autonomy period: indispensable for the nostalgic tourist or the historian. Reprinted as *Baedeker's Russia 1914*.

Modern guidebooks

89 **Travellers' guide: Finland.**

Sylvie Nickels. London: Cape, 1977. rev. ed. 240p. maps. bibliog.

A very good guide, with plenty of practical and background information. The descriptions of routes and places make up about half of the book.

90 **Finland: travel guide.**

Helsinki: Suomen turistineuvonta, 1979. 17th ed. 265p. maps.

An annual publication, which has also been entitled *Tourist guide Finland*. Contains some maps and general information, but the bulk of the guide is made up of entries for towns and tourist areas with good attention to hotels, restaurants and shops.

91 **Finland.**

Geneva: Nagel, 1980. 3rd rev. ed. 368p. maps. bibliog. (Nagel's Encyclopedia Guides).

Comprises an extensive introduction to Finland, followed by itineraries, and much practical information. Clear presentation.

92 **Finland: traveller's guide.**
Bengt Pihlström. Helsinki: Otava, 1971. 130p. map.

Much of the practical information is out of date but the 'Finland and the Finns' and 'Where to see what' sections remain worth reading. The author is head of the Finnish Tourist Board.

93 **Hints to business men: Finland.**
London: British Overseas Trade Board, 1978/79 [*sic*]. 52p. bibliog.

Excellent, brief, practical notes relating to the country, travel and, of course, economic information and import and exchange control regulations. Short but useful reading list of material in English on business conditions. Very good value, even for the non-business visitor. The next edition is to be entitled *Hints to exporters*.

Helsinki

94 **Finn guide to Helsinki.**
Gunilla Carlander, Camilla Bergendahl. Helsinki: Finnish Travel Association, 1979. 136p. maps. bibliog.

Compact, full of useful information, and up to date.

95 **Helsinki. Helsingfors. Arkkitehtuuriopas. Arkitektur guide. Architectural guide.**
Suomen rakennustaiteen museo. Finlands arkitekturmuseum. (Architectural Museum of Finland). Helsinki: Otava, 1976. 170p. maps.

This is a practical, pocket-sized guidebook. Introductory matter comprises 'A historical and architectural survey' and 'Post-war building in Helsinki'. Maps provide keys to the numbered list of buildings, which is divided geographically and which gives the architect and date of each building mentioned and sometimes a brief explanatory note. A number of black-and-white illustrations.

96 **Helsinki: a city in a classic style.**
Eino E. Suolahti. Helsinki: Ministry for Foreign Affairs & Otava, 1973. 63p.

Describes the building of Helsinki during the first decades of the autonomy period. Superbly illustrated with colour photographs and reproductions of old paintings and photographs.

97 **Vanha Helsinki. Det gamla Helsingfors. The old Helsinki. Le vieux Helsinki. Stary Khel'sinki. Das alte Helsinki.**
Markus Leppo. Helsinki: Valokuvakirja - Photobook, 1979. 113p.

A very brief historical introduction in six languages. Splendid photographs (coloured and black-and-white) with good captions.

98 **A journey to the northern capitals.**
Oliver Warner. London: Allen & Unwin, 1968. 157p.

Helsinki, p. 95-119. An evocative, personal view of the Finnish capital. The book also describes Copenhagen, Oslo and Stockholm.

Carl Ludvig Engel.
See item no. 649.

Carl Ludwig Engel: builder of Helsinki.
See item no. 650.

Prehistory, Archaeology and Ethnography

Prehistory and archaeology

99 **Finland.**
Ella Kivikoski. London: Thames & Hudson; New York: Praeger, 1967. 204p. maps. bibliog. (Ancient Peoples and Places, 53).

This, the only comprehensive scholarly work in English on Finland's prehistory, is an adaptation of the author's *Suomen esihistoria* (The prehistory of Finland) (Porvoo: Werner Söderström, 1961. VIII+310p.) which is a standard work on Finnish archaeology.

100 **Les anciens finnois.** (The ancient Finns.)
Aurélien Sauvageot. Paris: Klincksieck, 1961. 222p. map. bibliog.

A study of the origins and beginnings of the civilization of the Finns, using linguistic, archaeological, folklore and ethnographical sources. Divided into: Les origines lointaines; La civilisation matérielle; La vie sociale; La vie spirituelle. An appendix provides a survey of the development of ethnographical studies in Finland.

101 **Archaeology in Finland before 1920.**
Carl Axel Nordman. Helsinki: Societas Scientiarum Fennica, 1968. 82p. bibliog. (The History of Learning and Science in Finland 1828-1918, 14a).

One of a valuable series of books on the history of Finnish scholarship.

Ancient cultures of the Uralian peoples.
See item no. 102.

Early Finnish art from prehistory to the Middle Ages.
See item no. 592.

National Museum of Finland: guide.
See item no. 719.

Ethnography

102 **Ancient cultures of the Uralian peoples.**
Edited by Péter Hajdú. Budapest: Corvina, 1976. 336p. maps. bibliog.

Written by Hungarian and Finnish experts, the volume aims 'to give a concise, modern, clear and objective survey...of the most basic questions underlying the history of the Uralic peoples'. Part I: Linguistics; II: Archaeology and Anthropology; III: Material Culture; IV: Folk Art and Mythology. Contains much on the Finns and Finland, for example chapters on Finnish mythology by Anna-Leena Kuusi and on *Kalevala* and the [Estonian] *Kalevipoeg* by Väinö Kaukonen. Few of the references in the bibliographies are to works in western European languages.

103 **Suomen kansankulttuurin kartasto. Atlas der finnischen Volkskultur. Atlas of Finnish folk culture. 1. Aineellinen kulttuuri. Materielle Kultur. Material culture.**
Edited by Toivo Vuorela. Helsinki: Suomalaisen Kirjallisuuden Seura, 1976. 151p. maps. bibliog. (Suomalaisen Kirjallisuuden Seuran toimituksia [Publications of the Finnish Literature Society], 325).

An essential work for the study of ethnography in Finland. The eighty-four maps show the distribution of crafts, tool production, and types of buildings, furniture, tools, etc. The explanatory data is given in German or English as well as Finnish, with German predominating.

104 **The Finno-Ugric peoples.**
Toivo Vuorela. Bloomington, Indiana: Indiana University; The Hague: Mouton, 1964. v+392p. maps. bibliog. (Indiana University Publications Uralic and Altaic Series, 39).

An introductory chapter on 'The Finno-Ugric peoples in the light of philology' is followed by chapters on the different peoples, of which those on the Finns and the Lapps are of concern here. Particularly good on ethnography (Vuorela is a prominent Finnish ethnographer): livelihood, domestic animals, skis, building techniques and style, furnishings and handicrafts.

105 **Ethnology in Finland before 1920.**
Toivo Vuorela. Helsinki: Societas Scientiarum Fennica, 1977. 79p. bibliog. (The History of Learning and Science in Finland 1828-1920, 14b).

A concise history of its subject, concentrating on Finno-Ugric ethnology and the scholars and collectors in that field, but not neglecting Finland's general ethnologists.

106 **Tradition und Volkskunst in Finnland.** (Tradition and ethnography in Finland.)
Pirkko Sihvo. Helsinki: Museovirasto, 1978. 124p. map. bibliog.

A short introduction is followed by chapters on Finnish peasant farm buildings, their interiors and furnishings, food and drink, textiles, clothing, festivals and folk art. An English translation is in preparation.

107 **Finnish mills.**
Auvo Hirsjärvi, Rex Wailes. *Transactions of the Newcomen Society*, vol. XLI (1968-69), p. 85-101 and plates VIII-XIV; vol. XLIII (1970-71), p. 113-28 and plates XXI-XXX; vol. XLIV (1971-72), p. 99-118 and plates XV-XXI; vol. XLV (1972-73), p. 93-104 and plates XXI-XXVI.

Four articles describing Finnish watermills, mamsel or smock mills, hollow post mills, and post mills.

108 **Kansallispukuja.** (National costumes.)
Lahti, Finland: Helmi Vuorelma, 1978. 18p.

An illustrated pamphlet about Finnish national costumes, issued by a manufacturer of them, with a brief introduction (summarized in English) and an index of localities referring to the illustrations.

109 **Puukko: the Finnish knife.**
Eeva Siltavuori. *Look at Finland*, no. 5 (1973), p. 13-19.

An illustrated, popular account of the development of the Finnish *puukko* from a tool for woodcutting and a weapon for fighting into a modern all-purpose knife.

110 **Festival of summer and light.**
Anja Smolander. *Look at Finland*, no. 2 (1978), p. 38-45.

Describes modern and old Finnish midsummer customs. Bonfires are still lighted, some home decoration continues, and the Finnish flag is flown. In Swedish-speaking areas, maypoles take the place of bonfires.

111 **The peace of Christmas.**
Lea Venkula-Vauraste. *Look at Finland*, no. 4 (1978), p. 22-33.

An article for the general reader about Finnish Christmas customs, from Lucia Day and the *tierna* boys (players) to food, drink, trees and Father Christmas.

Les anciens finnois. (The ancient Finns.)
See item no. 100.

Finno-Ugric folk art.
See item no. 590.

The *ryijy*-rugs of Finland: a historical study.
See item no. 598.

The use and traditions of mediaeval rugs and coverlets in Finland.
See item no. 599.

Vaivaisukot. Finnish pauper sculptures.
See item no. 609.

Finland's wooden men-at-alms. Finlands fattiggubbar. Suomen vaivaisukot.
See item no. 610.

Talonpoikaistalot - talonpoikaisarkkitehtuurin katoavaa kauneutta. Bondgårdar - bondarkitekturens försvinnande skönhet. Peasant houses - the vanishing beauty of peasant architecture.
See item no. 632.

Finnish folk music.
See item no. 671.

Old Finnish folk dances.
See item no. 676.

Folk costumes and textiles.
See item no. 720.

Seurasaari ulkomuseo/open-air museum.
See item no. 721.

History

Finland as a part of Scandinavia

112 **A history of Scandinavia: Norway, Sweden, Denmark, Finland and Iceland.**
T. K. Derry. London: Allen & Unwin, 1979. x+447p. map. bibliog.

'Traces the history of the Scandinavian countries from the earliest times to the present day, emphasizing the common features in their inheritance from the past and in their contribution to the modern world.' Intended for readers with little prior knowledge of Scandinavia; bibliography of works in English.

113 **The northern tangle: Scandinavia and the post-war world.**
Rowland Kenney. London: Dent, 1946. xii+255p. maps.

A short history of the Scandinavian countries, emphasizing the period of the Second World War. Although generally dated, the basic outlook on the security policy 'tangle' of the northern countries remains relevant.

114 **The sea and the sword: the Baltic, 1630-1945.**
Oliver Warner. London: Cape; New York: Morrow, 1965. xiv+305p. maps. bibliog.

A bold attempt to outline the conflicts between the countries around the Baltic Sea.

115 **Scandinavian Journal of History.**
Stockholm: Almqvist & Wiksell, 1976- . quarterly.

Published under the auspices of the Historical Associations of Denmark, Finland, Norway and Sweden, to provide an opportunity for Nordic scholars 'to present to a wider international audience their investigations and the background evidence for their standpoints'.

116 **Excerpta Historica Nordica.**
Copenhagen: Gyldendal, 1955- .

The aim of this series, which is published under the auspices of the International Committee of Historical Sciences, is 'to make Scandinavian historical research accessible to an international public unable to read the Scandinavian languages'. Sections for Denmark, Finland, Norway and Sweden - and, from volume X, Iceland as well - are followed by a subject index and index of authors. Monographs published during the periods covered are summarized, sometimes quite extensively. The last volume published, in 1980, was vol. X, covering 1975-76.

117 **Scandinavian Economic History Review.**
Copenhagen: Scandinavian Society for Economic and Social History and Historical Geography, 1953- . semi-annual.

Comprises articles and reviews on the economic history of the Scandinavian countries and also an annual 'Select bibliography of contributions to economic and social history appearing in Scandinavian books, periodicals and year-books', 1967- . 'Contents I-XX, 1953-1972' was published in 1974.

General histories

118 **A history of Finland.**
Eino Jutikkala, Kauko Pirinen. London: Heinemann, 1979. new rev. ed. 256p. maps.

Originally published in 1962, this is largely a political history by two distinguished Finnish historians, in which all periods are given appropriate treatment. The detailed history ends with the immediate aftermath of the Second World War but this is supplemented by a brief 'Postwar chronicle'. Lacks a bibliography.

119 **A history of Finland.**
John H. Wuorinen. New York; London: Columbia University Press for the American-Scandinavian Foundation, 1965. xvii+548p. maps. bibliog.

This volume by an American historian concentrates on the period after 1917 and includes sections on economic and social developments. Appendices include the main articles of the peace treaties of 1920, 1940 and 1947, and the Treaty of Friendship, Cooperation and Mutual Assistance of 1948. Considerable select bibliography.

120 **Histoire de la Finlande.** (History of Finland.)
Aurélien Sauvageot. Paris: Imprimerie Nationale, 1968. 2 vols. map. (Bibliothèque de l'Ecole des Langues Orientales Vivantes, XXII).

A continuation of the author's *Les anciens finnois* (q.v.), this work deals with the period from the Middle Ages to 1961. Written for French students of the Finnish language.

121 **The political history of Finland 1809-1966.**
L. A. Puntila. Helsinki: Otava, 1974; London: Heinemann, 1975. 248p. maps.

A translation of a standard work by a former Professor of Political History in the University of Helsinki. Has no notes and no bibliography.

122 **Finland in the twentieth century.**
D. G. Kirby. London: Hurst, 1979. x+253p. map. bibliog.

By a British historian specializing in Finland, this is an important study and interpretation of Finnish history from the 1870s to the present, paying attention to economic and social developments as well as to politics. The concluding chapter on 'The Kekkonen era' surveys Finnish foreign policy since 1944, politics and society in the 1960s and 1970s, and examines the state of Finland today. The work embodies the results of recent Finnish and foreign research and has a good bibliography.

123 **Finland between East and West.**
Anatole G. Mazour. Princeton, New Jersey: Van Nostrand, 1956. Reprinted, Westport, Connecticut: Greenwood Press, 1976. xiv+298p. maps. bibliog.

An account of Finnish history - chiefly since 1899 - which emphasizes foreign, and in particular Finno-Russian, relations. 'The Appendix lists some of the most pertinent diplomatic documents of Soviet-Finnish relations since 1918.'

124 **Study in *sisu*.**
Austin Goodrich. New York: Ballantine, 1960. 144p. map.

A short, popular history of Finland - with particular emphasis on the Second World War period and its aftermath, up to the crisis of 1958 - and on the reasons why Finland is not a Soviet satellite.

125 **60 years independent Finland.**
Matti Klinge. Helsinki: Finnish-American Cultural Institute, 1977. 79p. maps.

An interesting historical essay by a leading Finnish historian, with a few pages on culture, and some good illustrations.

126 **In search of the past: approaches to Finnish history.**
Juhani Suomi. *Books from Finland*, vol. XIII, no. 4 (1979), p. 164-69. bibliog.

A convenient survey article of some recent (1978-79) publications on Finnish history and politics, by Finnish and foreign authors.

127 **Historiallinen aikakauskirja.** (Historical Journal.)
Helsinki: Suomen Historiallinen Seura & Historian Ystäväin Liitto, 1903- . quarterly.

A historical journal in Finnish containing articles on Finnish and general history, reviews, information about historians and their profession in Finland.

128 **Historisk tidskrift för Finland.** (Finnish Historical Journal.) Helsinki: Historiska föreningen, 1916- . quarterly.

A historical journal in Swedish, with articles, reviews, news of historical associations, archives and conferences, and an annual selected bibliography of books and articles on the history of Finland.

Suomen historian kartasto. Atlas of Finnish history.
See item no. 55.

Scandinavian atlas of historic towns.
See item no. 56.

Revue Internationale d'Histoire Militaire: Edition Finlandaise.
(International Review of Military History: Finnish Edition.)
See item no. 282.

A select list of books and articles in English, French and German on Finnish politics in the 19th and 20th century.
See item no. 762.

Finland: Books and Publications in Politics, Political History and International Relations.
See item no. 763.

Mediaeval and modern periods to 1917

129 **Medieval studies in Finland: a survey.**
Seppo Suvanto. *Scandinavian Journal of History*, vol. 4, no. 4 (1979), p. 287-304.

Material in English on Finnish mediaeval history is rare and this survey article of the work of Finnish mediaevalists is particularly welcome.

130 **Finland and Russia, 1808-1920, from autonomy to independence: a selection of documents.**
Edited by D. G. Kirby. London: Macmillan, 1975; New York: Barnes & Noble, 1976. xiv+265p. map. bibliog. (Studies in Russian and East European History).

Over 150 documents in translation, mostly from Finnish sources, on one of the central themes of Finnish history: the development of relations between Finland and Russia. Brief but good editorial comment.

131 **Nineteenth century nationalism in Finland: a comparative perspective.**
Risto Alapuro. *Scandinavian Political Studies*, n.s., vol. 2, no. 1 (1979), p. 19-29.

Compares Finnish nationalism with that arising among other nationalities in the 19th century multinational empires. Concludes that in Finland national consolidation and nationalism advanced calmly and steadily, a view not previously generally put forward.

132 **Nationalism in modern Finland.**
John H. Wuorinen. New York: Columbia University Press, 1931. x+303p. bibliog.

This major study of the development of Finnish and Swedish-Finnish nationalism in Finland up to 1920 remains worth reading.

133 **Nationalism and revolution: political dividing lines in the Grand Duchy of Finland during the last years of Russian rule.**
Osmo Jussila. *Scandinavian Journal of History*, vol. 2, no. 4 (1977), p. 289-309.

A valuable example of the work of a Finnish historian whose interpretations are free from the bias of post-1917 historiography in which events before Finland's independence have been seen with the hindsight of that independence.

134 **Autonomous Finland in the political thought of nineteenth century Russia.**
Keijo Korhonen. Turku, Finland: Turun yliopisto, 1967. 99p. bibliog. (Annales Universitatis Turkuensis, Ser. B, Tom. 105).

This work, which covers from the beginning of the autonomy period to the late 1880s, aims to explain the position held by Finland in the political thinking of politically influential groups in Russia and to show how those attitudes changed. It is based mainly on published material.

135 **The uneasy alliance: collaboration between the Finnish opposition and the Russian underground 1899-1904.**
William R. Copeland. Helsinki: Suomalainen Tiedeakatemia, 1973. 224p. bibliog (Annales Academiae Scientiarum Fennicae, Ser. B, Tom. 179).

A detailed, scholarly monograph on the evolution of cooperation between the Finns and the various Russian revolutionary groups.

136 **The Finnish Social Democratic Party and the Bolsheviks.**
David Kirby. *Journal of Contemporary History*, vol. 11, nos. 2 and 3 (1976), p. 99-113.

Shows how 'both the Finnish SDP and the Bolsheviks used each other's good offices without overmuch concern about closer understanding between the two' in the period 1905-17.

137 **The Finnish question in British political life, 1899-1914.**
George Maude. *Turun historiallinen arkisto* (Turku Historical Records), no. 28 (1973), p. 325-44.

The intensification of the Russo-Finnish constitutional and administrative conflict in 1899 was followed by a vigorous Finnish campaign to lobby for support in western Europe. Maude's article describes the efforts made in Britain, the attitude of British politicians towards those efforts, and the immovability of the British government which was more concerned with developing an understanding with Russia than with criticizing the illiberal Russian Finnish policy.

138 **Finland in Anglo-Russian diplomatic relations, 1899-1910.**
George Maude. *Slavonic and East European Review*, no. 113, vol. XLVIII (Oct. 1970), p. 557-81.

Describes how the efforts of the Finns to claim British attention to their problem had little effect on British relations with Russia.

The Republic

139 **The victors in World War I and Finland: Finland's relations with the British, French and United States governments in 1918-1919.**
Juhani Paasivirta. Helsinki: Finnish Historical Society, 1965. 198p. bibliog. (Studia Historica, 7).

'This work examines Finland's relations with the British, United States and French Governments during the closing stage of World War I and the period immediately after the war.' Based particularly on United States and Finnish archives.

140 **The winning of Finnish independence as an issue in international relations.**
Kalervo Hovi. *Scandinavian Journal of History*, vol. 3, no. 1 (1978), p. 47-73.

A useful survey of the attitude of the various powers to the question of Finland's independence in 1917-18.

141 **Lenin's nationality policy and Finland.**
Tuomo Polvinen. *Yearbook of Finnish Foreign Policy*, vol. 5 (1977), p. 3-8.

A careful examination of Lenin's view of nationality policy. Polvinen concludes that Lenin would have preferred to see Finland remain a part of Russia but since this could not be achieved by force he pressed for recognition of Finnish independence in accordance with his nationality policy.

142 **Finland and the Russian Revolution, 1917-1922.**
C. Jay Smith. Athens, Georgia: University of Georgia Press, 1958. [xii]+251p. maps. bibliog.

'An attempt...to trace Finland's relations with Russia from the beginning of Russification in 1899 to the end of the Finnish-supported insurrection of 1921-22 in Soviet Karelia.' Based on published sources only.

143 **Finland in British politics in the First World War.**
Eino Lyytinen. Helsinki: Suomalainen Tiedeakatemia, 1980. 219p. map. bibliog. (Annales Academiae Scientiarum Fennicae, Ser. B, Tom. 207).

'It is the main contention of this study that the British government was prepared to accept the new political constellation in the Baltic area, i.e. the disruption of the Russian Empire and the independence of Finland in early 1918, although the official recognition had to wait until the spring of 1919. The Finnish Civil War, the German intervention and the negative attitude of the United States government were responsible for this postponement.'

144 **The Aland [*sic*] Islands question: its settlement by the League of Nations.**
James Barros. New Haven, Connecticut; London: Yale University Press, 1968. xiii+362p. map. bibliog.

Describes the origin of the dispute between Finland and Sweden over the sovereignty of the Åland Islands and the role of the League of Nations in its subsequent settlement during the period 1917-21.

145 **In time of storm: revolution, civil war, and the ethnolinguistic issue in Finland.**
Pekka Kalevi Hamalainen. Albany, New York: State University of New York Press, 1979. xvii+172p. bibliog.

An examination, by an American historian, of 'the relationship of the critical revolutionary and civil war period, the Red and White cleavages and confrontation, and the causes and nature of the war itself to a major theme in nineteenth- and twentieth-century Finnish history - the ethnolinguistic juxtaposition of Finland's Finnish- and Swedish-speaking populations'. Considerable 'Selected bibliography'.

146 **Revolutionary ferment in Finland and the origins of the Civil War 1917-1918.**
D. G. Kirby. *Scandinavian Economic History Review*, vol. XXVI, no. 1 (1978), p. 15-35.

'The Finnish Civil War was not simply the result of events in Russia. It grew out of the increasingly desperate attempts of the Finnish working class to utilise a revolutionary situation, caused by the collapse of authority and the sudden deterioration of the economic situation...in order to obtain some alleviation of their situation and greater security for the future.'

147 **Red, White and Blue in Finland, 1918: a survey of interpretations of the Civil War.**
Ohto Manninen. *Scandinavian Journal of History*, vol. 3, no. 3 (1978), p. 229-49.

This article surveys the literature on the Civil War and considers the objectives and motives of the Reds and Whites, noting that the 'Blues' - those who stayed out of the conflict - have received little attention.

148 **Finland's War of Independence.**
J. O. Hannula. London: Faber & Faber, 1939. 2nd ed. 229p. maps.

A military history of the Finnish Civil War of 1918 written from the White standpoint by a Finnish officer who previously produced a larger Finnish work on the subject. Useful as an account of operations.

149 **Communist parties of Scandinavia and Finland.**
Anthony F. Upton, with contributions by Peter P. Rohde, Å. Sparring. London: Weidenfeld & Nicolson, 1973. x + 422p. bibliog. (The History of Communism).

150 **Communism in Scandinavia and Finland: politics of opportunity.**
Anthony F. Upton, with contributions by Peter P. Rohde, Å. Sparring. Garden City, New York: Anchor Press/Doubleday, 1973. x+422p. bibliog.

This work and the preceding item are the same book with different titles. Three short essays on the communist parties of Denmark, Norway and Sweden precede Upton's chapters which constitute a detailed study of the Communist Party of Finland from its origins to the mid-1960s.

151 **Communism in Finland: a history and interpretation.**
John H. Hodgson. Princeton, New Jersey: Princeton University Press, 1967. xi+261p. bibliog.

A major account and evaluation of communism in Finland from the rise of socialism to the election of 1945.

152 **Finland.**

Anthony F. Upton. In: *European fascism.* Edited by S. J. Woolf. London: Weidenfeld & Nicolson, 1968, p. 184-216.

A very good survey of the growth and decline of fascism in Finland, pointing out that it owed its strength to local, native roots and not to the ideology of international fascism.

153 **Three generations: the extreme right wing in Finnish politics.**

Marvin Rintala. Bloomington, Indiana: Indiana University Press, 1962. [viii]+281p. bibliog. (Indiana University Publications. Russian and East European Series, 22).

An important study of the Finnish extreme right during the period 1918-39. The concept of political generation is used to illuminate, *inter alia*, the ideal of Greater Finland, the Lapua Movement (which aimed to eradicate communism in Finland), the influence of the army and the Civil Guards (a volunteer military organization), and the influence of the Academic Karelia Society (a Finnish nationalist and russophobic organization of students and teachers).

154 **Finland.**

Marvin Rintala. In: *The European right: a historical profile.* Edited by Hans Rogger, Eugen Weber. London: Weidenfeld & Nicolson, 1965, p. 408-22.

On the political thought, action and organization of the extreme right in Finland during the years 1917-39.

155 **The Lapua Movement: the threat of rightist takeover in Finland, 1930-1932.**

Risto Alapuro, Erik Allardt. In: *The breakdown of democratic regimes.* Edited by Juan J. Linz, Alfred Stepan. Baltimore, Maryland; London: Johns Hopkins University Press, 1978, p. 122-41.

Considers the cleavages in Finnish society arising from the Civil War and developments preceding it, as well as immediate political and economic developments in the period 1929-32, as factors contributing to or hampering the success of the Lapua Movement.

156 **Right-wing radicalism in Finland during the inter-war period: perspectives from and an appraisal of recent literature.**

Jorma Kalela. *Scandinavian Journal of History*, vol. 1, nos. 1 and 2 (1976), p. 105-24.

Examines particularly the work of Marvin Rintala and Risto Alapuro, looking at the rise and decline of the Lapua Movement and at the IKL (Patriotic People's Movement), its successor.

157 **Finnish military politics between the two world wars.**
William J. Stover. *Journal of Contemporary History*, vol. 12, no. 4 (1977), p. 741-57.

Considers that from 1918 to 1932 the Finnish armed forces acted in collaboration with the extreme right to attempt to expand Finnish territory and crush Marxism and parliamentary democracy, but that their failure to coerce the government caused civilian control to emerge over the armed forces after 1932.

Folklore and nationalism in modern Finland.
See item no. 512.

The Second World War

158 **Conflict in the north: recent writings on the Winter War (1939-1940).**
David G. Kirby. *Books from Finland*, vol. X, nos. 3 and 4 (1976), p. 59-63.

A useful review article which examines some of the contrasting views of the Winter War between the Soviet Union and Finland which have been presented in recent Finnish works.

159 **The development of Finnish-Soviet relations during the autumn of 1939, including the official documents.**
Finland. Ministry for Foreign Affairs. London: Harrap, 1940. 114p. maps.

This remains a useful collection of documents in translation, presenting the Finnish version of events leading up to the Winter War.

160 **Finland 1939-1940.**
Anthony F. Upton. London: Davis-Poynter, 1974. 174p. maps. bibliog. (The Politics and Strategy of the Second World War).

The best short account of the Winter War in English, well-written and based on a sound understanding of the sources. Good selective bibliography.

161 **The white death: the epic of the Soviet-Finnish Winter War.**
Allen F. Chew. East Lansing, Michigan: Michigan State University Press, 1971. xi+313p. maps. bibliog.

This book concentrates mainly on military operations and is more detailed than the other accounts in English. It is well thought of in Finnish military circles.

162 **The Winter War: Russia against Finland.**
Richard W. Condon. London: Pan/Ballantine, 1972. 160p. maps. bibliog. (The Pan/Ballantine Illustrated History of World War II).

A short, popular account of the Winter War, concentrating on military operations. Good illustrations.

163 **The Winter War: Finland October 5, 1939 - March 13, 1940.**
Anthony F. Upton. In: *History of the Second World War*. London: Purnell, 1966, vol. 1, no. 5, p. 123-40. maps.

A concise illustrated account of the Winter War.

164 **The Winter War: the Russo-Finnish conflict, 1939-40.**
Eloise Engle, Lauri Paananen. London: Sidgwick & Jackson; New York: Scribner's, 1973. xv+176p. maps. bibliog.

A very popular account of the war, mostly about military events.

165 **The diplomacy of the Winter War: an account of the Russo-Finnish War, 1939-40.**
Max Jakobson. Cambridge, Massachusetts: Harvard University Press, 1961. [ix]+281p. map. bibliog.

Describes the diplomatic background to the Winter War, the attitude of the great powers to the war, and the diplomatic activity of the Finnish government during the war.

166 **The Winter War: Finland against Russia, 1939-1940.**
Väinö Tanner. Stanford, California: Stanford University Press, 1957. x+274p. map.

Tanner, a leading Finnish Social Democrat politician, describes in this book the negotiations in Moscow in which he took part before the outbreak of the Winter War, and then Finland's efforts to make peace with the Soviet Union, efforts which he led as foreign minister in the government formed after the war had begun.

167 **The appeal that was never made: the Allies, Scandinavia and the Finnish Winter War, 1939-40.**
Jukka Nevakivi. London: Hurst, 1976. [xii]+225p. map. bibliog.

A considered historical study of Allied politics and plans during the Winter War which has made use of British, Swedish, Norwegian, Finnish and French archives. The author sees Finland as only an object in the policy-making of the great powers.

168 **Three days to catastrophe.**

Douglas Clark. London: Hammond, 1966. 228p.

A popular account of Allied plans for intervention in Finland during the Winter War and of how the Allies avoided war with the Soviet Union by three days - when Finland made peace. It is important to note that the book was published before the British archives were opened for research.

169 **Finland in international politics: the great powers and the Nordic countries 1939-1940.**

Tuomo Polvinen. *Scandinavian Journal of History*, vol. 2, nos. 1 and 2 (1977), p. 107-22.

Considers political cooperation between Finland and the Nordic countries before, during and after the Winter War.

170 **America and the Russo-Finnish War.**

Andrew J. Schwartz. Washington, DC: Public Affairs Press, 1960. vii+103p.

'This study examines the course, the nature, and the objectives of American foreign policy toward Finland and the Soviet Union during the critical years from 1939 to 1944.' It is based on extensive use of US Department of State records.

171 **Finland in crisis, 1940-41: a study in small-power politics.**

Anthony F. Upton. London: Faber & Faber, 1964; Ithaca, New York: Cornell University Press, 1965. 318p. maps. bibliog.

One of the most significant and crucial periods of Finnish history lies between the end of the Winter War with the Soviet Union in March 1940 and the resumption of hostilities following the German invasion of the USSR in June 1941. Upton's book does not claim to be a definitive account of Finnish policy during this period but it has been a seminal work on the subject. Hitherto Finnish scholars had argued that Finland had drifted willy-nilly into war in 1941; Upton's argument that Finland was a willing participant in German plans to attack the Soviet Union aroused intense controversy in Finland.

172 **Finland in the Second World War.**

C. Leonard Lundin. Bloomington, Indiana: Indiana University Press, 1957. ix+303p. map. bibliog.

This book concentrates on Finland's relations with Germany and the Soviet Union and is frank in its discussion of Finnish involvement in war in 1941 and of Finnish war aims. Its impact in Finland was less than that of Upton's *Finland in crisis* (see preceding entry) but it started the debate on Finnish involvement in war in 1941. It covers a longer period than Upton's book.

173 **Finland and World War II, 1939-1944.**

Edited by John H. Wuorinen. New York: Ronald Press, 1948. iv+228p. maps.

Published for an anonymous Finn, now known to have been the Finnish historian Professor Arvi Korhonen, this book sets forth the Finnish side of how Finland became involved in the war. Somewhat disingenuous, it remains an interesting period piece. The argument that 'Finland's "war guilt"...does not grow out of situations or actions Finland herself deliberately willed' has not been unchallenged.

174 **Finland, Germany, and the Soviet Union, 1940-1941: the Petsamo dispute.**
H. Peter Krosby. Madison, Wisconsin; London: University of Wisconsin Press, 1968. xvii+276p. map. bibliog.

The question of the ownership and exploitation of the nickel mines in the Finnish territory of Petsamo caused great difficulties for the Finns in 1940-41 since it exposed them to British, German and Soviet pressure. Finnish nickel proved a vital means of obtaining German support against Soviet demands and Krosby argues that the Petsamo question served as an accurate barometer of Finland's relations with Germany in 1940-41.

175 **Finland's entrance into the Continuation War.**
Mauno Jokipii. *Yearbook of Finnish Foreign Policy*, vol. 5 (1977), p. 8-19.

A carefully documented article by a leading Finnish military historian on how Finland became involved in the Continuation War of 1941-44 with the Soviet Union, the 'continuation' being of the Winter War.

176 **Finland's foreign policy 1940-1941: an ongoing historiographic controversy.**
Kent Forster. *Scandinavian Studies*, vol. 51, no. 2 (1979), p. 109-23.

This article reviews the stormy course of historical writing about Finland's entry into the war with the USSR in 1941 and concludes that the argument that Finland drifted into the war is no longer tenable but that the debate is not yet over.

177 **Barbarossa: the Finnish front. Finland/USSR, June/December 1941.**
Anthony F. Upton. In: *History of the Second World War.* London: Purnell, 1967, vol. 2, no. 10, p. 713-17. map.

A concise account of the background to Finnish involvement in the war against the Soviet Union in 1941 and, in greater detail, of Finnish operations to the end of December 1941.

178 **End of the Arctic war: Finland, June/October 1944.**
Anthony F. Upton. In: *History of the Second World War.* London: Purnell, 1968, vol. 5, no. 16, p. 2225-32. map.

Carries the story of the Finnish campaign from early 1942, through the crisis of the Soviet offensive of June 1944 to the eventual Finnish rally and defensive victory on the Karelian Isthmus, the retreat from Eastern Karelia, and the armistice of September 1944. Concludes with Soviet operations in Petsamo and north Norway to the end of October 1944.

179 **The last Finnish war.**
Waldemar Erfurth. Washington, DC: University Publications of America, 1979. [vii]+253p. (Classified Studies in Twentieth-Century Diplomatic and Military History).

This is a shortened translation of *Der finnische Krieg 1941-1944* (Wiesbaden, GFR: Limes Verlag, 1950. 324p.), whose author, a German general, was representative of the German High Command at Finnish General Headquarters during the Continuation War, and whose account of operations and relations with Mannerheim is worth reading. Unfortunately the translation is marred by the misleading practice of writing the Finnish letters *ä* and *ö* as *ae* and *oe*, while the maps and index of the original have been omitted.

180 **The power of small states: diplomacy in World War II.**
Annette Baker Fox. Chicago: University of Chicago Press, 1959. [xi]+212p. bibliog.

Of especial interest here is chapter III, 'Finland: fighting neutral', p. 43-77, which summarizes the diplomatic history of the war as it affected Finland. Suggests that Finnish experience illustrates the circumstances under which a small power cannot resist the pressure of one or more great powers during war without becoming involved in violence, but notes also the influence of Finnish decisions on the course of events: thus the Germans failed in their attempts to use the Finns against Leningrad and the Murmansk railway.

181 **Treaty of Peace with Finland, Paris, 10th February, 1947.**
London: HM Stationery Office, 1948. 123p. map. (Cmd. 7484. Treaty Series, No. 53 [1948]).

The full text (in English, Russian, French and Finnish) of the peace treaty between the USSR, the United Kingdom, other Allies, and Finland.

182 **Finland.**
Anthony F. Upton. In: *Communist power in Europe, 1944-1949.* Edited by Martin McCauley. London: Macmillan, 1977, p. 133-50.

The volume examines the events of 1944-49, concentrating on the activities of the various communist parties. Upton's chapter on Finland suggests that the communists in Finland did not fail to seize power in 1948 - as they did in all other East European countries within the Soviet sphere of influence - because they did not intend to do so. Stalin could get what he wanted more advantageously in Finland through the conservative J. K. Paasikivi, who was first Prime Minister and then President, than through the Finnish Communist Party.

Finland's war years 1939-1945: a list of books and articles concerning the Winter War and the Continuation War, excluding literature in Finnish and Russian.
See item no. 764.

Biographies and memoirs

183 **Four Finns: political profiles.**
Marvin Rintala. Berkeley, California: University of California Press, 1969. [ix]+120p.

This book compares and analyses the political careers of four major Finnish leaders: Gustaf Mannerheim (a conservative soldier who was twice head of state), Väinö Tanner (a Social Democrat who held numerous ministerial appointments), K. J. Ståhlberg (a liberal constitutional lawyer and the republic's first president), and J. K. Paasikivi. Rintala concludes that of these Paasikivi (a conservative banker and president in 1946-56) 'expressed the highest aspirations of the Finnish people'.

184 **Svinhufvud, the builder of Finland: an adventure in statecraft.**
Erkki Räikkönen. London: Alan Wilmer, 1938. vii+252p.

Pehr Evind Svinhufvud (1861-1944) was a lawyer and conservative politician who became head of state in 1918 and president of the republic in 1931-37. This book is a sympathetic account of his involvement in the stormy events of 1917-18 which captures the atmosphere of the time as it appeared to the Finnish Whites.

185 **The memoirs of Marshal Mannerheim.**
Carl Gustaf Emil Mannerheim. London: Cassell, 1953; New York: Dutton, 1954. xi+540p. maps.

Baron Gustaf Mannerheim was one of the dominating personalities in Finland during the period from 1918 to 1946, a soldier with a keen political sense and, at times, great influence on national policy. His *Memoirs*, abridged in English, convey his interpretation of modern Finnish history while discreetly revealing little of himself.

186 **Marshal Mannerheim and the Finns.**
Oliver Warner. London: Weidenfeld & Nicolson, 1967. 232p. map. bibliog.

This is the only biography of Mannerheim in English which covers the whole of his life. Warner succeeded very well in portraying the character of the man.

187 **Mannerheim: the years of preparation.**
J. E. O. Screen. London: Hurst, 1970. ix+158p. maps. bibliog.

Describes Mannerheim's early life and service as an officer in the imperial Russian army before he returned to Finland and achieved fame as the victor in the Civil War of 1918. Looks also at the development of writing about Mannerheim and has a good bibliography.

188 **Gustaf Mannerheim and Otto W. Kuusinen in Russia.**
Marvin Rintala, John H. Hodgson. *Slavonic and East European Review*, vol. 56, no. 3 (July 1978), p. 371-86.

Describes the very divergent careers in Russia of two Finns of totally different political complexions. Kuusinen, one of the leaders of the Red side in the Finnish Civil War of 1918, left at the end of the war for Soviet Russia, where he helped form the Finnish Communist Party, and held important positions in the Comintern and the Central Committee of the Communist Party of the Soviet Union.

189 **J. K. Paasikivi: a pictorial biography.**
Uuno Tuominen, Kari Uusitalo. Helsinki: Otava, 1970. 101p.

Despite its title, this book is not simply made up of pictures. It has a reasonable text which gives an outline assessment of the life and work of Juho Kusti Paasikivi (1870-1956), the Finnish banker and statesman whose lasting achievement was the establishment of good relations between Finland and the Soviet Union after the Second World War.

190 **The Paasikivi line.**
John H. Hodgson. *American Slavic and East European Review*, vol. XVIII, no. 2 (April 1959), p. 145-73.

Examines the salient features of Paasikivi's activity and thought, his role in the crisis of 1948, when a communist *coup* in Finland seemed likely, and his attitude to relations with the Soviet Union - the 'Paasikivi line' itself.

191 **Urho Kekkonen: a statesman for peace.**
Edited by Keijo Korhonen. Helsinki: Otava, 1975. 186p.

An important series of articles in which a number of Finnish and Scandinavian authorities examine the influence and ideas of President Kekkonen relating to various aspects of Finnish foreign policy and international relations.

192 **A far-sighted leader with a sense of purpose.**
Kustaa Vilkuna. *Look at Finland*, no. 1 (1978), p. 2-5.

This article by the late academician Vilkuna, a friend of President Kekkonen, describes the reelection of the president for his fifth term in office, his background and career. The title harmonizes with the tone of the article.

193 **Finland and the great powers: memoirs of a diplomat.**
Georg Achates Gripenberg. Lincoln, Nebraska: University of Nebraska Press, 1965. xx+380p.

Georg Achates Gripenberg (1890-1975) was successively Finnish envoy to London, the Vatican and Stockholm during the Second World War. His memoirs, based on his diaries, give an important, inside picture of Finnish policies and attitudes.

Population

Statistics and general studies

194 **Väestönlaskenta. Folkräkningen. Population census. 1970.**
Helsinki: Tilastokeskus, 1973-76. Vols. I-XIX. (Suomen virallinen tilasto. Finlands officiella statistik. Official Statistics of Finland, VI. C: 104).

Volume I contains 'General demographic data', and XIX the 'List of tables'; the detailed information appears in the intermediate volumes, in which English introductions and vocabularies facilitate use by foreigners. Finland has had decennial censuses since 1950, although population statistics through the parish registers go back to 1749 and these were taken on a ten-year basis from 1880.

195 **Väestöntutkimuksen vuosikirja. Yearbook of Population Research in Finland.**
Helsinki: Population Research Institute, 1946- .

Published as *Väestöliiton vuosikirja* (Yearbook of the Finnish Population and Family Welfare League) from 1946 to 1956 (vols. 1-5), the yearbook concentrates on demographic developments, population and family welfare policy. From vol. 11, 1969, the yearbook has been published entirely in English. It contains articles, surveys and reviews, and regular bibliographies of Finnish population research.

196 **The population of Finland: a World Population Year monograph.**
Helsinki: Central Statistical Office, 1975. 81p. (Committee for International Coordination of National Research in Demography Series).

Prepared by the Finnish Central Statistical Office in cooperation with the Population Research Institute, this book examines recent population development (with a look back at development since the beginning of the 18th century), and includes surveys on the development of the labour force, on projections relating to manpower and education, and on the effects of economic and social policy on population development.

197 **Fertility and mortality in Finland since 1750.**

Oiva Turpeinen. *Population Studies: a Journal of Demography*, vol. 33, no. 1 (March 1979), p. 101-14.

Considers the general features of the development of fertility and mortality, how they are linked with economic factors, particularly crop fluctuations, population shifts in Finland, and family planning. The general statistics cover from 1751 to 1975 but the appended tables of age-specific mortality rates and of age-specific fertility rates cover 1751-1925.

198 **The Finnish population structure: a genetic and genealogical study.**

H. R. Nevanlinna. *Hereditas*, vol. 71 (1972), p. 195-235. maps. bibliog.

This study of the distribution of both polymorphic and rare marker genes in the Finnish rural population shows evidence of the effect of genetic drift maintained by national and local isolation. Indications are that the breeding unit has been small up to the present time. The distribution of a variety of very rare genes, which is limited to areas first settled in prehistoric times, is taken as evidence that all the early Finns used the same route of immigration across the Gulf of Finland rather than separate eastern and western routes. It should be added that this is a controversial question.

199 **Report of the Committee on the Position of Women in Finnish Society.**

Helsinki: Government Printing Centre, 1973. 155+16p. (Report of the Committee 1970: A 8).

This is an English version of an extensive report submitted in 1970 by a committee set up by the government in 1966 'to study the position of women in Finnish society, to carry out the necessary research and to draw up plans and recommendations for the improvement of the position of women'. It covers child-rearing and education, women in working life, the family, and participation in public affairs. An appendix explains legislative reforms which took place in 1970-72 after the report was issued.

200 **Naisten asema. Kvinnornas ställning. Position of women.**

Helsinki: Tilastokeskus, 1980. 207p. (Tilastollisia tiedonantoja. Statistiska meddelanden. Statistical Surveys, 65).

Provides statistical information on the position of women, including education, income, family and children, and health. The statistical data was collected in 1977-78.

201 **Finnish youth.**
Edited by Antti Marttinen. Vaasa, Finland: Civic Education Centre, 1977. 30p. (Publications of the Civic Education Centre, 29).

Very bare information about study, work, housing and leisure. Rather more useful is a classified list of youth organizations (p. 21-30). A new edition is in preparation.

Finland Swedes

202 **Finland.**
In: *Linguistic minorities in western Europe.* By Meic Stephens. Llandysul, Wales: Gomer Press, 1976, p. 267-93. map. bibliog. (p. 750-51).

Provides a summary of the history, size, legal and cultural position of 'The Swedish Finnlanders', 'The Åland Islanders', and 'The Lapps of Lake Inari'.

203 **Finns and Swedes as minorities in Sweden and Finland.**
Erik Allardt. *Scandinavian Review*, vol. 66, no. 1 (March 1978), p. 17-23.

Allardt distinguishes four distinct minority groups: Swedish-speaking Finns, Finnish-speaking people in Sweden's Lapland, Finnish-speaking Finns who emigrated to Sweden after the Second World War, and Swedish-speaking Finns who emigrated to Sweden after the Second World War. He examines the differences between these groups, both in historical origin and in their degree of bilingualism and identification with the country in which they live.

204 **[Swedish culture in Finland].**
Adult Education in Finland, vol. 11, no. 2 (1974), 32p. bibliog.

The entire issue is devoted to Swedish culture in Finland and comprises the following articles which together afford a good introduction to the Finland Swedes: 'The Swedes in Finland', by Aimo Halila; 'Finland's Swedish speaking population as a minority and an ethnic group', by Erik Allardt; 'The legal situation of the Swedish population in Finland', by Tore Modeen; 'The Swedish school system in Finland', by Carl-Erik Thors; and 'The Finland-Swedish cultural life observed with eyes of an author', by Lars Huldén.

205 **Finland's Swedish speaking minority.**
Erik Allardt. Helsinki: Research Group for Comparative Sociology, University of Helsinki, 1977. [i]+21p. bibliog. (Research Reports, 17).

A very interesting, if brief, account of the legal status of the Finland Swedes, their historical background, socioeconomic composition as part of the population of Finland, and factors influencing the decrease in their numbers. Concludes that the social structure is remarkably similar in the Finnish- and Swedish-speaking populations.

206 **Changes in the social structure of the Swedish-speaking population in Finland, 1950-1970.**
Karl Johan Miemois. Helsinki: Research Group for Comparative Sociology, University of Helsinki, 1978. [i]+37p. maps. bibliog. (Research Reports, 19).

Shows that although there are no really great differences between the Finnish-speaking and Swedish-speaking populations when comparing social stratification, a higher proportion of administrative and clerical employees is found among Swedish-speakers, and there is a corresponding under-representation of manual workers in the Swedish-speaking population. These differences are accentuated by regional contrasts.

207 **The situation of the Finland-Swedish population in the light of international, constitutional and administrative law.**
Tore Modeen. *McGill Law Journal*, vol. 16, no. 1 (1970), p. 121-39.

Modeen argues that the Finland-Swedish population as a whole lacks the protection of international law. The protection given by the constitution is dependent on the willingness of the Finnish majority to respect the principle of equality in the question of language and cultural rights, but major wrongs have been avoided since the nationally-based Swedish People's Party has acted as a watchdog for the minority. Very few cases have occurred in recent years concerning observance of the language regulations. Modeen concludes that because of their relatively large numbers and their position as contacts between Finland and other Nordic countries where Finnish is not known, Swedes in Finland can vindicate the retention of their linguistic and cultural rights.

208 **The international protection of the national identity of the Åland Islands.**
Tore Modeen. *Scandinavian Studies in Law*, vol. 17 (1973), p. 175-210.

A summary of the question of sovereignty over the Åland Islands and more particularly of the origin and status of the agreement of 27 June 1921 containing guarantees for the preservation of the Islands' Swedish national character. There is a full discussion and analysis of the problems concerning the international guarantees for the protection of the national identity of the Islands. Appendices contain extracts from various relevant documents.

Lapps

209 **The Lapps in Finland: the population, their livelihood and their culture.**
Eino Siuruainen, Pekka Aikio. Helsinki: Society for the Promotion of Lapp Culture, 1977. [ii]+60p. maps. bibliog. (Society for the Promotion of Lapp Culture Series, No. 39).

A handy introduction to the Lapps as one of a number of circumpolar minority peoples. In the Nordic countries the Lapps are beginning to establish a common international identity and to become involved in the investigation of problems concerning the areas where they live.

210 **The Lapps.**
Roberto Bosi. London: Thames & Hudson, 1960. 220p. maps. bibliog. (Ancient Peoples and Places, 17).

The inclusion of the Lapps in the series is justified by the fact that they are an ancient people surviving into modern times. Describes early information about them, how they live, what they believe, and discusses the problem of Lapp origins. Select bibliography, mostly of works in English; other references are in the notes to the various chapters.

211 **The Lapps.**
Björn Collinder. New York: Greenwood Press, 1969. [x]+252p. maps. bibliog.

Reprint of a work originally published in 1949. A very good general study covering the history, life, religion, literature, art and music of the Lapps as a whole.

212 **The Lappish nation: citizens of four countries.**
Karl Nickul. Bloomington, Indiana: Indiana University, 1978. xiv+134+[214]p. maps. bibliog. (Indiana University Publications. Uralic and Altaic Series, 122).

About the way of life of the Lapps and how it varies in different areas, the attitudes of the countries concerned towards the Lapps, and how the Lapps have organized themselves and have been organized. A large and excellent selection of illustrations.

213 **The Lapps.**
Arthur Spencer. New York: Crane, Russak; Newton Abbot, England: David & Charles, 1978. 160p. map. bibliog. (This Changing World).

Describes where the Lapps live, the Lapps in history, the significance of the reindeer to them, Lapp society, beliefs, language, literature, music and art, and how the Lapps are being affected by the modern world. Extensive select bibliography, mostly of works in English.

214 **The Skolt Lapps today.**
Tim Ingold. Cambridge, England: Cambridge University Press, 1976. xi+276p. maps. bibliog.

An anthropologist's study of the present condition of the Skolt Lapps who were evacuated from the Petsamo region in 1939-40 and finally resettled in Finnish Lapland near the Norwegian frontier. Good bibliography and guide to further reading on the Lapps.

215 **The "Lappish movement" and "Lappish affairs" in Finland and their relations to Nordic and international ethnic politics.**
Ludger Müller-Wille. *Arctic and Alpine Research*, vol. 9, no. 3 (Aug. 1977), p. 235-47. bibliog.

An interesting account of how 'ethnic awareness' has developed and been developed among the Lapps and how the responses of the Finnish government have had the effect of creating 'more possibilities for an ambitious elite of Lappish politicians to promote their ideas'.

The Finns and the Lapps: how they live and work.
See item no. 22.

The Finno-Ugric peoples.
See item no. 104.

Finland.
See item no. 202.

Gypsies

216 **Blood feuding among Finnish gypsies.**
Martti Grönfors. Helsinki: Department of Sociology, University of Helsinki, 1977. [vii]+iii+193p. bibliog. (Research Reports, 213).

The author comments that 'on the whole, Finnish gypsies have received remarkably little attention from sociologists and anthropologists....There seems to be a general assumption that Finland has only two ethnic minorities, the Lapps and the Swedish-speaking Finns'. As well as a descriptive study of the blood feud, this book includes a valuable little history of Finnish gypsies (p. 14-33) and a section on gypsy society in Finland (p. 34-84).

Emigration

217 **External migration of the Finns in the 1970's.**
Altti Majava. *Väestöntutkimuksen vuosikirja. Yearbook of Population Research in Finland,* vol. XV (1977), p. 46-64.

A detailed article, making use of published and unpublished statistics, reviewing the characteristics of emigration and return migration, their causes and consequences for Finland and for Sweden, the principal destination of modern Finnish migration.

218 **Maassamuutto sekä Suomen ja Ruotsin välinen muuttoliike 1950-1975. Inrikes omflyttning samt omflyttning mellan Finland och Sverige 1950-1975. Internal migration and migration between Finland and Sweden in 1950-1975.**
Pekka Myrskylä. Helsinki: Tilastokeskus, 1978. x+161p. (Tilastokeskus. Statistikcentralen. Central Statistical Office of Finland. Tutkimuksia. Undersökningar. Studies No. 48. Muuttoliike. Omflyttning. Migration. 1950-1975).

Reports on the development of internal migration and emigration to the Scandinavian countries between 1950 and 1975 and studies what sort of people migrated. Summary in English; explanations of figures and tables in English.

219 **Migration from Finland to Russia during the nineteenth century.**
Max Engman. *Scandinavian Journal of History*, vol. 3, no. 2 (1978), p. 155-77.

An authoritative survey of the main features of Finnish emigration to European Russia during the 19th century, noting especially the influence exerted on Finnish migration by the city of St. Petersburg.

220 **Migration from Finland to North America in the years between the United States Civil War and the First World War.**
Reino Kero. Turku, Finland: Turun yliopisto, 1974. [vii]+260p. bibliog. (Annales Universitatis Turkuensis, B, 130).

This Turku University thesis describes the causes of Finnish emigration to North America and the mechanics of the operation. It distinguishes two long-term cycles in Finnish migration (1874-93 and 1894-1914), shows that almost all emigrants were from rural districts, and most were men. The book, with the same title, has been reprinted by the Institute for Migration, Turku, as Migration studies, C 1.

221 **Finnish immigrants in America, 1880-1920.**
A. William Hoglund. Madison, Wisconsin: University of Wisconsin Press, 1960. ix+213p. maps. bibliog.

An account of where the immigrants came from and why, how they organized themselves, their occupations, politics, and sense of belonging in America. Extensive notes; the section on sources includes a good bibliography.

222 **Old friends - strong ties.**
Edited by Vilho Niitemaa, Jussi Saukkonen, Tauri Aaltio, Olavi Koivukangas. Turku, Finland: Institute for Migration, 1976. 349p.

Compiled in honour of the United States Bicentennial. The articles, by various authors, are gathered into three parts: A: Emigration from Finland to America; B: Finnish-American life; C: Finland and the United States in 1917-1976.

Finns and Swedes as minorities in Sweden and Finland.
See item no. 203.

Religion

223 **Scandinavian churches: a picture of the development and life of the churches of Denmark, Finland, Iceland, Norway and Sweden.**

Edited by Leslie Stannard Hunter. London: Faber & Faber, 1965. 200p. bibliog.

Most chapters are by Scandinavian churchmen. The book is partly put together on a systematic basis (e.g. 'Church and people', 'Worship and liturgy'), and partly on a country basis. There is a brief section on 'The relationship of church and state in Finland' by Bishop Erkki Kansanaho, but there is much of value in other chapters, too.

224 **Kyrkan i Finland. The church in Finland. Die Kirche in Finnland.**

Maunu Sinnemäki. Helsinki: Kirjaneliö, 1978. 40p.

These extremely brief notes in Swedish, English and German on the church in Finland have the virtue of being fairly up to date.

225 **The church in Finland.**

Maunu Sinnemäki. Helsinki: Otava, 1973. 64p.

Covers briefly but informatively the history, organization, creeds and dogmas, ministers, and life and work of the Lutheran Church of Finland. Adds a note on other Christian churches in Finland.

226 **Finland: its church and its people.**

Geert Sentzke. Helsinki: Luther-Agricola Society, 1963. 212p. bibliog.

An account of the Lutheran Church of Finland, its history, administration, doctrine and work.

227 **The Finnish church at work.**
Anne Fried. *Look at Finland*, no. 1 (1975), p. 14-19.

A very brief account for the general reader of the relationship between the state and the Lutheran Church, followed by an account of the committees of the church and their functions.

228 **Proud heir of a glorious tradition.**
Anja Smolander, Kimmo Smolander. *Look at Finland*, no. 1 (1974), p. 36-45.

Describes - and illustrates magnificently - the Orthodox monastery at Heinävesi in eastern Finland, the continuation of the great tradition of the famous Russian monastery of Valamo in Lake Ladoga.

229 **800 years of Orthodox faith in Finland.**
Lea Venkula-Vauraste. *Look at Finland*, no. 5 (1977), p. 42-47.

A well illustrated, popular article about the Orthodox Church in Finland, its history, organization, and the New Valamo Monastery.

Art treasures of the Eastern Orthodox Church of Finland in the Kuopio Orthodox Church Museum.
See item no. 594.

Society

Social policy and conditions

230 **Social policy for the sixties: a plan for Finland.**
Pekka Kuusi. Helsinki: Finnish Social Policy Association, 1964. 295p. maps.

This is a somewhat abridged version of Kuusi's seminal work *60-luvun sosiaalipolitiikka*, which appeared in 1961 and which has had an influence in Finland, it is said, comparable to that of the Beveridge Report in Britain. It examines the aims of public policy, the role of social policy, specific aspects of social policy (e.g. manpower, housing, public health, social assistance), and how social policy could be financed and coordinated. The author is a political scientist and Social Democrat politician.

231 **The means and aims of Finnish social policy.**
Väestöntutkimuksen vuosikirja. Yearbook of Population Research in Finland, vol. XVI (1978), p. 17-40.

A useful group of articles by different authors on, respectively: Family policy; Social and health policy: focus and development; Housing policy and population development; Manpower policy in Finland; The effects of population factors on educational planning; Regional policy and population development.

232 **In the shadow of the factory: social change in a Finnish community.**
Patricia Slade Lander. New York: Schenkman, 1976. xii+191p. maps. bibliog.

A social anthropologist's study of a community of 2,800 people in North Savo, based on field work carried out in 1967-68. The emphasis of the book is on the influence on the community of the local pasteboard factory and social change.

233 **Social sources of Finnish communism: traditional and emerging radicalism.**
Erik Allardt. *International Journal of Comparative Sociology*, vol. V, no. 1 (1964), p. 49-72.

Allardt shows that Finnish communism is both 'industrial' (in developed areas) and 'backwood' (in insecure environments measured in terms of unemployment and housing conditions), the latter being emerging radicalism, where communist support was increasing in unstable conditions.

Social services, health and welfare

234 **Finland: a Scandinavian modern country.**
Kaarina Jousimaa. Helsinki: Finnish-American Cultural Institute, 1978. 79p.

This brief, illustrated introduction to Finland concentrates on the various aspects of social welfare.

235 **Social security in Finland.**
Jaakko Pajula, Esko Kalimo. *International Social Security Review*, vol. 32, no. 2 (1979), p. 160-73.

This is a description of the administration of social security in Finland, sickness insurance, pension insurance, unemployment and accident insurance, and social expenditure and its financing. The article has been reprinted by the Research Institute for Social Security of the Social Insurance Institution, Helsinki, 1980.

236 **Pension schemes in Finland 1977.**
Insurance in Finland, no. 1 (1978), p. 5-20.

An extensive article on the various pension schemes in force in Finland, their conditions, and the amounts paid. Part of a report by Margaretha Aarnio and Jouko Janhunen of the Central Pension Security Institute entitled *Pensions schemes in various countries in 1977* and published in Finland in 1977.

237 **Child welfare in Finland.**
Helsinki: Central Union for Child Welfare, 1977. 2nd rev. ed. 53p. (Central Union for Child Welfare Publication, 44).

Contains a great deal of information in a small compass about the organization of child welfare, the allowances and assistance available to families and children, about children in need of care and protection, and arrangements for the care and rehabilitation of the handicapped, disturbed and delinquent.

238 **The national housing programme for 1976-1985.**
Ilkka Puro. *Bank of Finland Monthly Bulletin*, vol. 50, no. 10 (Oct. 1976), p. 20-26.

Presents a broad outline of the first Finnish national housing programme, designed to provide a framework for housing policies in 1976-85. Surveys basic targets, volume of housing, demands on construction, and the financing and implementation of the programme.

239 **Social welfare and health services in Finland: labour protection and legislation.**
Helsinki: Ministry of Social Affairs and Health, 1977. 32p.

A short, official guide to labour protection legislation in Finland. It outlines how labour protection is administered; the state of the law as regards working conditions, accidents and occupational diseases; and planned legislation in this field.

240 **Social welfare and health services in Finland: social welfare and social allowances.**
Helsinki: Ministry of Social Affairs and Health, 1976. 40p. bibliog.

Outlines the organization of the Ministry of Social Affairs and Health, the National Board of Social Welfare, and local authorities, which together have the main responsibilities in the field covered by the pamphlet. Describes the different types of social welfare available - from holiday relief for farmers to discharge benefit for national servicemen - and the social allowances payable.

241 **Health services in Finland.**
Helsinki: Ministry of Social Affairs and Health, National Board of Health, 1979. 32p.

A brief description of the health situation in Finland (healthy babies and sick men), the administration of health care, dentistry and hospitals.

242 **Primary health care in Finland.**
Helsinki: Ministry of Social Affairs and Health, National Board of Health, 1978. 28p. bibliog.

The Primary Health Care Act of 1972 provides for a network of health centres run by the local authorities to promote health and provide treatment. This pamphlet describes the background to the act and how it works. Good visual presentation of statistics.

243 **Finland's health policy.**
Kari Puro. *Bank of Finland Monthly Bulletin*, vol. 49, no. 8 (Aug. 1975), p. 20-23.

Shows that the mortality rates of Finns are notably higher than those in other Nordic countries. High standard hospitals have not raised the state of health noticeably. Describes the goals of present health policy, which are to allocate more resources to the prevention of diseases and to primary health care.

244 **One hundred years of war and peace: Finnish Red Cross 1877-1977.**
Gunnar Rosén. Helsinki: Suomen Punainen Risti, 1977. 26p.

A short account of the history and present organization and activities of the Finnish Red Cross.

Crime

245 **Major fluctuations in crimes of violence in Finland: a historical analysis.**
Heikki Ylikangas. *Scandinavian Journal of History*, vol. 1, nos. 1 and 2 (1976), p. 81-103.

Ylikangas, a historical criminologist, argues that the incidence of crimes of violence has fluctuated and that this discredits explanations based on the character of the people (e.g., see the following entry). He sees high rises in the incidence of criminality as an expression of social protest.

246 **Homicides and suicides in Finland and their dependence on national character.**
Veli Verkko. Copenhagen: G. E. C. Gads Forlag, 1951. 189p. maps. bibliog. (Scandinavian Studies in Sociology, 3).

The excellent and long-collected Finnish statistics on homicides and suicides are analysed, and the author concludes that the great frequency of crimes against life in Finland 'is due to the natural inclination, or disposition, of Finns towards unpremeditated crimes of violence, manslaughter and assault. This disposition is connected with a poor ability to hold alcohol....It is perhaps the most important expression of the negative aspect of Finnish "sisu" [perseverance]'. The author considers that poor ability to carry liquor 'may not be a morbid but an entirely normal property, arising from a known type of physical structure'. Verkko's views have been challenged, for example by Ylikangas (see preceding item).

Alcohol policy

247 **Alcohol policy and the consumption of alcohol beverages in Finland in 1951-1975.**
Salme Ahlström-Laakso, Esa Österberg. *Bank of Finland Monthly Bulletin*, vol. 50, no. 7 (July 1976), p. 20-28.

An extensive survey of the activities of the state alcohol monopoly, Alko, between 1951 and 1975. Includes comments on the policy line of favouring light beverages and on the heavy consumption of alcohol in the 1970s, which is now considered to be a serious public health problem.

248 **Alcohol and the Finns.**
Ingalill Österberg. *Look at Finland*, no. 1 (1977), p. 56-58.
The presence of drunks and alcoholics is quickly apparent to visitors to Finland. This short article describes Finnish drinking habits and the treatment available for alcoholism in Finland.

249 **Drinking and driving in Helsinki.**
M. Mäki, M. Linnoila, A. Alha. *Accident Analysis and Prevention*, vol. 9, no. 3 (Sept. 1977), p. 183-89.
Summarizes the legislation on drinking and driving and the role of alcohol in traffic accidents in Finland. Examines a sample of breath-tested drivers in Helsinki and concludes that the very punitive Finnish legislation on drinking and driving, which is probably generally effective, is ineffective in dealing with repeated offenders.

250 **The prohibition experiment in Finland.**
John H. Wuorinen. New York: Columbia University Press, 1931. x+251p. bibliog.
Finland had prohibition from 1919 until the beginning of 1932. This book surveys the background to the law - the temperance movement in Finland - and the consequences of prohibition: the problems of drunkenness, crime, alcoholism and the cost of prohibition enforcement. The law was repealed following a referendum; the book makes reference to its proponents and opponents in the final sections.

Politics and Government

Constitution and parliament

251 **Constitution Act and Parliament Act of Finland.**
Helsinki: Ministry for Foreign Affairs, 1967. 85p.
English translations of the Constitution Act (1919) and the Parliament Act (1928). These are preceded by an introductory chapter 'The Finnish constitutional system and its development' by Paavo Kastari, a constitutional lawyer.

252 **The planned constitutional reform in Finland.**
Ilkka Saraviita. *Scandinavian Studies in Law*, vol. 22 (1978), p. 135-47.
Describes the historical background of the Finnish constitution of 1919 and the Parliament Act of 1928, the attitudes towards them of the political parties, and discussions on reforms, concentrating on the work of the constitutional committees set up in 1977.

253 **The Finnish parliament.**
Jyväskylä, Finland: Gummerus, 1979. 95p. bibliog.
Contains short but authoritative articles by various authors on the history of parliamentary institutions in Finland, the unicameral legislature, the parliament today, the role of parliament in international relations, and on the parliament building as an architectural structure. Handsome illustrations show both the old building completed in 1931 and the extension dating from the late 1970s.

La protection des droits de l'homme en droit constitutionnel finlandais.
(The protection of human rights in Finnish constitutional law.)
See item no. 276.

Civil and political rights in Finland.
See item no. 277.

The protection of economic, social and cultural rights in Finland.
See item no. 278.

Political system

254 **The Finnish political system.**
Jaakko Nousiainen. Cambridge, Massachusetts: Harvard University Press, 1971. x+454p. map. bibliog.

This is a good introduction to the structure of Finnish society, Finnish political parties, the institutions of government (central and local), and how the political system works. Extensive bibliography.

255 **The electoral system of Finland.**
Klaus Törnudd. London: Evelyn, 1968. 181p. bibliog.

Describes the origins and working of the Finnish parliamentary electoral system of proportional representation. The tables of election results are useful for reference and the 'Bibliographical note' (p. 174-78) is a helpful essay on the literature of the subject.

256 **All-party government for Finland?**
David Arter. *Parliamentary Affairs*, vol. XXI, no. 1 (winter 1978), p. 67-85.

A detailed discussion of a proposal by Johannes Virolainen, then chairman of the Centre Party, in March 1977 for an amendment to the constitution to provide for permanent all-party government. Nothing has come of the proposal but this article is a useful survey of the Finnish political system and parties.

257 **An election in Finland: party activities and voter reactions.**
Pertti Pesonen. New Haven, Connecticut; London: Yale University Press, 1968. xix+416p.

An examination by a leading political scientist of the 1958 election, comprising an account of the election campaign and voting behaviour in the city of Tampere and the rural district of Korpilahti, using interviews and analyses of newspaper contents.

258 **The 1978 Finnish presidential elections.**
Robert Wihtol. *Yearbook of Finnish Foreign Policy*, vol. 5 (1977), p. 59-65.

Examines the themes of the 1978 presidential elections, noting the emphasis on foreign policy. Provides voting figures.

259 **The 1979 election in Finland: good-bye to the 1970s.**
Pertti Pesonen, Matti Oksanen. *Scandinavian Political Studies*, n.s., vol. 2, no. 4 (1979), p. 385-97.

Discusses the results of the 1979 election and examines party support and changes in voting.

260 **The Finnish election of 1979: the empty-handed "winner"?**
David Arter. *Parliamentary Affairs*, vol. XXXII, no. 4 (autumn 1979), p. 422-36.

Looks particularly at the National Coalition (Kokoomus) conservative party, which did very well in the general election of March 1979. However, the conditions of Finnish multiparty coalitions are such that a broad centre-left government was again formed after the election, leaving the conservatives empty-handed.

261 **The political regions of Finland.**
Onni Rantala. *Scandinavian Political Studies*, vol. 2 (1967), p. 117-40.

Examines the support for various political parties or groups in different parts of Finland and concludes that a highly developed regionalism is characteristic of the 'political map' of Finland.

262 **Scandinavian Political Studies: a Journal Published by the Nordic Political Science Association: Denmark, Finland, Iceland, Norway and Sweden.**
Oslo: Universitetsforlaget, vols. 1-12, 1966-77; new series, 1978- . quarterly.

Publishes articles, review articles and reviews on political science, with particular emphasis on Scandinavia. The last volume of the old series, 12, 1977, is on 'Political science in the Nordic countries 1960-1975' and includes articles on 'The political science profession in Finland', by Pertti Pesonen (p. 29-45), and 'Political science in Finland 1960-1975: from behaviouralism to policy analysis', by Dag Anckar (p. 105-26).

A select list of books and articles in English, French and German on Finnish politics in the 19th and 20th century.
See item no. 762.

Finland: Books and Publications in Politics, Political History and International Relations.
See item no. 763.

Political parties

263 **Finland.**

Bengt Matti. In: *Communism in Europe: continuity, change and the Sino-Soviet dispute. Volume 2.* Edited by William E. Griffith. Cambridge, Massachusetts; London: MIT Press, 1966, p. 371-410.

Contains a brief account of how the Finnish Communist Party (SKP) fits into the Finnish political scene, and of Finno-Soviet relations since the 1950s. This precedes a longer history of the party with particular reference to the effects of the Sino-Soviet dispute on the party and on the Democratic Union of the Finnish People (SKDL), within which the SKP is the major force. There is an appendix on the organization of the party, its officials, and allied and front organizations.

264 **Finnish communism and electoral politics.**

John H. Hodgson. *Problems of Communism*, vol. XXIII, no. 1 (Jan.-Feb. 1974), p. 34-45.

A useful article explaining the factors behind the post-war strength of the Finnish Communist Party, the weakness of social democracy, and the reasons for the setback to the left wing in the 1970 elections.

265 **The popular front in Finland.**

Pertti Hynynen. *New Left Review*, no. 57 (Sept.-Oct. 1969), p. 3-20.

The inclusion of the Finnish Communist Party in the government of Finland, in what is described here as a 'popular front coalition', is seen as a result of the peculiarities of the Finnish political system together with the new structural problems of Finnish capitalism. The author concludes that the coalition has in no way modified the capitalist system and has prompted a split in the Finnish Communist Party itself.

266 **The Finnish Social Democratic Party.**

Ralf Helenius. In: *Social democratic parties in western Europe.* Edited by William E. Patterson and Alastair H. Thomas. London: Croom Helm, 1977, p. 272-87.

An account of the place of this important party in the party system, its participation in government, its structure and cohesion, and future goals.

267 **The Finnish Christian League: party or 'anti-party'?**

David Arter. *Scandinavian Political Studies*, vol. 3, no. 2 (1980), p. 143-62.

The Finnish Christian League (Suomen Kristillinen Liitto) did well in the 1979 general election. This article looks at how this non-socialist 'protest' party has mobilized support and at who its activists are.

Social sources of Finnish communism: traditional and emerging radicalism.
See item no. 233.

The Finnish election of 1979: the empty-handed "winner"?
See item no. 260.

Local government

268 **Local and regional self-government in Finland.**
Local Finance: International Bimonthly Journal, vol. 8, no. 1 (Feb. 1979), p. 21-24.

A short summary of how local government works in Finland; the article was originally published in *Information Bulletin*, no. 13 (first quarter 1978) of the Council of Europe, and is based on Finnish sources.

The Finnish political system.
See item no. 254.

Law and the legal system

269 **The Finnish legal system.**
Edited by Jaakko Uotila. Helsinki: Union of Finnish Lawyers, 1966. 263p. bibliog.

Seventeen chapters by a number of legal specialists about different aspects of Finnish law, including the system of national and local government as well as the law relating to particular subjects. A useful description, helped by short bibliographies of Western-language books and an index.

270 **Law and lawyers in Finland.**
Helsinki: Union of Finnish Lawyers, 1975. 3rd ed. 16p.

A very brief but informative pamphlet mentioning the number of lawyers, the requirements for the practice of law, legal education, the courts and judges.

271 **Suomen laki.** (The law of Finland.)
Helsinki: Suomen Lakimiesliitto, 1978-79. 2 vols.

The Union of Finnish Lawyers first published this systematic collection of laws in 1955. It is a comprehensive collection of the most important statutes in force. A new revised edition of each volume is published every two years. Volume I (1979) deals with civil, commercial and criminal law, Volume II (1978) with administrative law. A Swedish language collection, on the same lines, has been published since 1963: *Finlands lag* (The law of Finland), (Helsinki: Finlands Juristförbund, 1978. XXXII+2331+28p.).

272 **Suomen asetuskokoelma.** (The collected laws of Finland.)
Helsinki: Suomen asetuskokoelma, 1860-

Also published in Swedish: *Finlands författningssamling* (Helsinki: Finlands författningssamling, 1860-). The titles vary. The collection is published throughout the year and has an annual chronological index and an annual subject index. Cumulated indexes cover 1860-89, 1890-1909, 1910-19, 1920-31, 1932-37, 1938-50 (Swedish), 1938-44, 1945-50 (Finnish), 1951-60, 1961-70. The series was preceded by *Samling af placater, förordningar, manifester och påbud* (Collection of edicts, decrees, manifestos and ordinances) (Turku: Helsinki, 1821-62, 17 vols.) covering 1808-59, and *Samling af de till efterlefnad gällande bref, förklaringar och föreskrifter* (Collection of letters, declarations and instructions currently in force) (Helsinki, 1836-52, 7 vols.) covering 1809-59. There is an index to these: *Sakregister till Finlands författningssamling: hänförande sig till Författnings- och Brefsamlingarne från år 1808 till år 1860* (Subject index to the collected laws of Finland, referring to the collections of laws and letters from 1808 to 1860) (Helsinki, 1876). Treaties are published in a separate series: *Suomen asetuskokoelman sopimussarja: ulkovaltain kanssa tehdyt sopimukset* (Swedish: *Finlands författningssamlings fördragsserie: överenskommelser med främmande makter*) (Treaty series of the collected laws of Finland: treaties concluded with foreign states). This is published throughout the year and has an annual index. The treaty series has covered treaties concluded since 1918 and has been published, with varying titles, since 1925.

273 **The Supreme Administrative Court and the Finnish system of application of the law.**
Helsinki: Supreme Administrative Court, 1976. 15p.

This booklet provides a summary of the system of courts in Finland with particular emphasis on the administrative courts as distinct from the civil and criminal courts, which comprise the other main division of the system. The administrative branch of the court system has jurisdiction over all decisions made in the administrative field.

274 **The ombudsman in Finland: the first fifty years.**
Mikael Hidén. Berkeley, California: Institute of Governmental Studies, University of California, 1973. xvi+198p. bibliog.

This condensed version of the author's *Eduskunnan oikeusasiamies* (The parliamentary ombudsman) (1970) is a comprehensive treatment of the constitutional background, the office of the ombudsman, his jurisdiction, origins of cases, actions and publicity for his work. There are statistical appendices of complaints and cases.

275 **The parliamentary ombudsman in Finland: position and functions.**
Helsinki: Office of the Parliamentary Ombudsman, 1976. rev. ed. 40p. bibliog.

Describes the position and functions of the Finnish parliamentary ombudsman, with translations of the relevant laws and regulations, and statistics of cases.

276 **La protection des droits de l'homme en droit constitutionnel finlandais.** (The protection of human rights in Finnish constitutional law.)
Tore Modeen. *Revue des Droits de l'Homme. Human Rights Journal*, vol. 8, no. 1 (1975), p. 201-14.

Provides a brief survey of Finnish constitutional development culminating in the constitution of 1919 and describes how that constitution protects human rights in practice.

277 **Civil and political rights in Finland.**
Toivo Sainio. *Revue des Droits de l'Homme. Human Rights Journal*, vol. 8, no. 1 (1975), p. 215-20.

Considers briefly the relevant provisions of the constitution of 1919.

278 **The protection of economic, social and cultural rights in Finland.**
Mikael Hidén. *Revue des Droits de l'Homme. Human Rights Journal*, vol. 8, no. 1 (1975), p. 275-81.

Looks particularly at what economic, social and cultural rights are protected at constitutional level.

279 **The police of Finland.**
Helsinki: Finnish Chapter of the International Police Association in collaboration with the Department for Police Affairs of the Ministry of the Interior, [1978?]. 38p.

An information booklet about the history, organization and training of the police.

Finnish press laws.
See item no. 726.

Defence forces

280 **Finnish national defence.**
Helsinki: General Headquarters' Information Section, 1978. 44p. maps.

This is a clear presentation of the official concept of Finnish security policy and the duties, organization and training of the defence forces. It also provides some notes on economic defence, civil defence (which is taken seriously in Finland), and United Nations peacekeeping activities in which Finnish troops have been involved. Good graphical presentation of, for example, the phases of training officers and non-commissioned officers, and good photographs of modern equipment.

281 **Report of the Second Parliamentary Defence Committee, Finland.**
Helsinki: Ministry of Defence, 1976. 56p. (Committee Report 1976: 37).

This report of a committee composed chiefly of members of parliament offers some insight into Finnish security policy and the factors taken into account in formulating that policy and in interpreting it in a practical way through the defence forces.

282 **Revue Internationale d'Histoire Militaire: Edition Finlandaise.**
(International Review of Military History: Finnish Edition.) Helsinki: Comité International des Sciences Historiques, Commission d'Histoire Militaire Comparée, 1961. no. 23. 103-273p. bibliog.

The entire issue is devoted to Finland and its articles - in French or English - deal with several important aspects of Finnish military history. There is an extensive bibliographical essay by Yrjö Aav, p. 258-72.

283 **The defence forces of Finland: supplement to the *Army Quarterly and Defence Journal.***
Tavistock, England: West of England Press, 1974. 40p.

Produced in full cooperation with the Finnish Ministry of Defence and the defence forces, and consisting of articles by senior Finnish officers, this pamphlet gives a useful - though now rather dated - outline of the role, history, training and equipment of the Finnish army, navy, air force and frontier guard. Also includes a section on Finnish participation in United Nations peacekeeping operations.

284 **Finnish Air Force 1918-1968.**
Christopher F. Shores, Richard Ward. Canterbury, England: Osprey Publications, 1969. 52p. (Aircam Aviation Series, S2).

This is a short history of the Finnish Air Force, giving information about its organization and aircraft, together with accounts of operations during the Winter and Continuation Wars. There are excellent black-and-white photographs of the wide range of aircraft used, as well as coloured drawings of several types, showing camouflage and markings, to which particular attention is paid in the text and from which aircraft modellers would derive considerable benefit. Appendices list aircraft acquired in the Winter War, aircraft strengths in the Continuation War, and top-scoring pilots.

Guide to the Military Archives of Finland.
See item no. 717.

Medals

285 **Les ordres nationaux de la Finlande.** (The national orders of Finland.)
Klaus Castrén. Helsinki: Ministère des Affaires Etrangères, 1975. 70p.

Gives the regulations of the three Finnish orders of chivalry: the Cross of Freedom, the White Rose of Finland, and the Lion of Finland, illustrations of them, and the order of precedence of decorations in Finland. Short introduction on the history and design of these orders.

Suomessa käytetyt rahat. Mynt och sedlar använda i Finland. Coins and banknotes used in Finland.
See item no. 287.

Postage stamps, numismatics

286 **Stamps of Sweden and Finland: the earlier issues.**
Ernest H. Wise. London: Heinemann, 1975. viii+168p. bibliog. (Heinemann Philatelic Series, 6).

The section on Finland, p. 99-161, is divided into 'The "Primitive" stamps', 'The enlightened years 1875-1901', and 'The Russian designs'; it thus covers the autonomy period to 1917. Considerable detail is given of the different stamps in use, their printing, perforation and usage.

287 **Suomessa käytetyt rahat. Mynt och sedlar använda i Finland. Coins and banknotes used in Finland.**
Edited by Erkki Borg. Helsinki: Pohjoismainen Kirja, 1976. 2nd rev. ed. 656p. bibliog.

A large format and large-scale work on Finnish coins and notes, with numerous illustrations, and appendices on Finnish medals and medallic art. Extensive bibliography. Gives prices. It is not fully academic in its character but is so large as to be almost comprehensive. A vocabulary is provided to help use the descriptions but the descriptive material appears in English as well as Finnish and Swedish.

Foreign Relations

General

288 **The Finnish dilemma: neutrality in the shadow of power.**
George Maude. London: Oxford University Press for the Royal Institute of International Affairs, 1976. vi+153p. bibliog.

A concise, informative and reliable study of Finnish foreign policy, with particular emphasis on Finnish-Soviet relations and on Finnish neutrality.

289 **Yearbook of Finnish Foreign Policy 1973-**
Helsinki: Finnish Institute of International Affairs, 1974-

Aims 'to give a representative account of the central issues of Finnish foreign policy during the year under review'. Contains articles, speeches and documents about Finnish foreign policy and incorporates a chronology of events. The contributors include politicians, civil servants, diplomats and scholars. Many of the articles were originally published in *Ulkopolitiikka* (Foreign Policy), the journal of the Finnish Institute of International Affairs. Essential reading on its subject.

290 **Essays on Finnish foreign policy.**
Vammala, Finland: Finnish Political Science Association, 1969. 114p.

A very important collection of essays: 'Finland's security policy', by Aimo Pajunen; 'Finland and the Soviet Union', by Keijo Korhonen; 'The problem of Germany in current Finnish foreign policy', by Hannu Vesa; 'Finland in the United Nations during the 1960s', by Klaus Törnudd; 'Finland as a member of the Nordic community', by Göran von Bonsdorff; 'Finland and external assistance', by Jaakko Iloniemi; 'Finland and regional economic integration in western Europe', by Erkki Mäentakanen; 'Finland's international cultural relations', by Kalervo Siikala; 'The parliament of Finland and foreign policy decision-making', by Bengt Broms. Succeeds a volume of essays, *Finnish foreign policy*, published by the Association in 1963 (see the following item).

291 **Finnish foreign policy: studies in foreign politics.**
Helsinki: Finnish Political Science Association, 1963. 232p. bibliog.

Fourteen articles, by authoritative writers, on foreign policy before and after Finnish independence, Finland's treaties and other agreements, reparations, commercial policy, Finland and international organizations, foreign policy decision-making, neutrality, and the parties and the press and foreign policy. Differs in character from the subsequent collection published by the association, *Essays on*

Finnish foreign policy (see the preceding item), and has not been entirely superseded with the passage of time.

292 **Finnish neutrality: a study of Finnish foreign policy since the Second World War.**
Max Jakobson. London: Evelyn, 1968; New York: Praeger, 1969. 116p. map.

An interesting, if controversial, account by a leading Finnish diplomat.

293 **The survival of small states: studies in small power-great power conflict.**
David Vital. London: Oxford University Press, 1971. vii+136p.

Chapter 4, 'Finland - a paradigm for the future', p. 99-117, stresses the 'now traditional and well-understood forms of loose and indirect control over Finnish affairs' and argues that closer control would be counter-productive to Soviet interests in northern Europe. This is the opposite of the argument of the 'Finlandizers'.

294 **Neutrality: the Finnish position. Speeches by Dr Urho Kekkonen, President of Finland.**
Urho Kekkonen. London: Heinemann, 1973. expanded ed. 258p.

A selection of speeches by Kekkonen over the period 1943 to 1972 which set out his views on Finnish foreign policy.

295 **Urho Kekkonen and postwar Finnish foreign policy.**
Jukka Nevakivi. *Yearbook of Finnish Foreign Policy*, vol. 3 (1975), p. 6-20.

A rather detailed and well-documented study of Kekkonen's foreign policy, its evolution and consequences, by a diplomatic historian.

296 **The foreign policy of President Urho Kekkonen.**
Keijo Korhonen. *Contemporary Review*, vol. 227, no. 1317 (Oct. 1975), p. 194-97.

A very brief note of the aims and characteristics of Kekkonen's foreign policy by a senior Foreign Ministry official who has also served as foreign minister.

297 **Finland and détente: self-interest politics and Western reactions.**
H. Peter Krosby. *Yearbook of Finnish Foreign Policy*, vol. 6 (1978), p. 40-45.

Krosby, a historian specializing on Finland, argues that, from a Finnish perspective, Finland has not gone further in the Soviet direction than it need, that the frequent reassurances of Finnish loyalty are necessary, and that Western suspicions of Finlandization are unjustified.

298 **Nuclear-weapon-free areas, zones of peace and Nordic security.**
Osmo Apunen. *Yearbook of Finnish Foreign Policy*, vol. 6 (1978), p. 2-19.

One of five articles on arms control in northern Europe contained in this issue of the *Yearbook*. Apunen, a leading Finnish foreign policy analyst, describes three 'waves' in the Finnish policy-makers' idea of a Nordic nuclear-weapon-free zone: 1962-65, 1972-75 and May 1978. He argues for the disengagement of the great powers from the Nordic region.

299 **The future of a nuclear-weapon-free zone in northern Europe.**
Yuri Komissarov. *Yearbook of Finnish Foreign Policy*, vol. 6 (1978), p. 26-31.

Komissarov is the pseudonym of a Soviet expert on Finland. This article expresses the Soviet line on a Nordic nuclear-weapon-free zone, a favourable view effectively nullified by the refusal of the Soviet Union to include any of its own territory in that zone.

300 **Finland, Comecon and the EEC.**
F. Singleton. *The World Today*, vol. 30, no. 2 (Feb. 1974), p. 64-72.

This article describes why Finland's attempt to come to terms with the European economic realities represented by the EEC was so controversial: namely, the need to safeguard Finnish commercial interests without implying any change in foreign policy, particularly towards the USSR.

301 **Finland's economic relations with developing countries in the light of development cooperation and trade policy.**
Vilho Harle. *Yearbook of Finnish Foreign Policy*, vol. 6 (1978), p. 45-53.

A survey of Finnish development cooperation policy, aid and trade and Finland's attitude to the New International Economic Order.

302 **A survey of foreign language literature on Finnish foreign policy.**
Heimo Vesala. *Yearbook of Finnish Foreign Policy*, vol. 2 (1974), p. 63-66.

An introductory, selective survey of studies of Finland's post-war foreign policy in languages other than Finnish. Includes books and articles in Scandinavian languages, English, Russian, French and German. Individual items are not annotated but there are useful comments at the beginning of each section.

Urho Kekkonen: a statesman for peace.
See item no. 191.

Suomen asetuskokoelma. (The collected laws of Finland.)
See item no. 272.

With Scandinavia

303 **The reluctant Europeans: the attitudes of the Nordic countries towards European integration.**
Toivo Miljan. London: Hurst, 1977. viii+325p. bibliog.

'This book is about the Nordic countries' relations with an integrating Europe during the three decades since the Second World War.' It looks at the questions of security and of economics in relation to the Nordic countries in general and in particular, and stresses the desire of all the Nordic countries to conserve the nation in the form of a sovereign independent state, a desire which has made them reluctant to integrate with each other, let alone with Europe.

304 **The Nordic Council: a study of Scandinavian regionalism.**
Stanley V. Anderson. Stockholm: Svenska Bokförlaget/Norstedts, 1967. xvi+194p. bibliog. (Scandinavian University Books).

Attempts 'to describe and explain Scandinavian regionalism by illuminating its most prominent organ, the Nordic Council'. Describes cooperation as the keynote of Scandinavian regionalism. Appendix of documents (e.g. the statute of the Nordic Council) and a select bibliography of works in major western European languages. Still useful as background.

305 **The Nordic Council and Scandinavian integration.**
Erik Solem. New York; London: Praeger, 1977. [xii]+199p. map. bibliog. (Praeger Special Studies in International Politics and Government).

Concentrates on the Nordic Council as the central driving force in Nordic cooperation, considering how it works and what it does. The author concludes that the Scandinavian countries appear to be more integrated, even economically, than any other group of independent states in the world, and that several impressive results have been achieved without the element of a supranational organization.

306 **Economic relations in the Nordic area: failures and achievements.**
Lauri Karvonen. *Yearbook of Finnish Foreign Policy*, vol. 5 (1977), p. 52-59.

Looks at Nordic economic relations since the Second World War, in particular in relation to Finland. Sees Sweden and Norway as centres of capital; Finland and Denmark as sources of labour.

With the Soviet Union

307 **The Treaty of Friendship, Cooperation and Mutual Assistance: historical background and present significance.**
Urho Kekkonen. *Yearbook of Finnish Foreign Policy*, vol. 1 (1973), p. 32-36.

A speech by the President to mark the twenty-fifth anniversary of the Treaty of Friendship, Cooperation and Mutual Assistance between the Soviet Union and Finland. This treaty is the cornerstone of Finland's foreign policy and this is a convenient statement of Kekkonen's views about it as 'the charter of our peace-loving policy of neutrality'.

308 **Silk glove hegemony: Finnish-Soviet relations, 1944-1974. A case study of the theory of the soft sphere of influence.**
John P. Vloyantes. Kent, Ohio: Kent State University Press, 1975. xiii+208p.

Considers Soviet-Finnish relations between 1944 and 1974 as a case study of the 'soft sphere of influence' theory, whereby influence on a country is indirect and sovereignty more real than nominal. The author concludes that there is such a phenomenon as a soft sphere of influence. The book's historical account of Soviet-Finnish relations is of more interest in the context of this bibliography than is its theoretical basis.

309 **Self-censorship in Finland.**
Carl-Gustaf Lilius. *Index on Censorship*, vol. 4, no. 1 (1975), p. 19-25.

An article by a Finnish writer and journalist describing 'self-censorship', the state of affairs by which statements regarded as harmful to the Soviet Union are not published in Finland. Lilius argues that self-censorship is harmful to Finland and makes more difficult the establishment of good neighbourly relations with the Soviet Union. The article caused considerable controversy in Finland.

310 **Conflicts in Finnish and Soviet relations: three comparative case studies.**
Raimo Väyrynen. Tampere, Finland: Tampereen yliopisto, 1972. 270p. (Acta Universitatis Tamperensis, Ser. A, Vol. 47).

Investigates 'the conflict factors which have appeared in Finnish-Soviet relations in 1948-1949, 1958-1959 and 1961-1962'. Contains a great deal of theory but also some interesting material on the Soviet Union's Finnish policy.

311 **Geographical and political factors in Finland's relations with the Soviet Union.**
Osmo Apunen. *Yearbook of Finnish Foreign Policy*, vol. 5 (1977), p. 20-31.

Examines territorial questions relating to Finland from the point of view of Soviet local, regional and global security.

312 **The Finnish-Soviet Long-term Programme - a chart for co-operation.**
Kari Möttölä. *Yearbook of Finnish Foreign Policy*, vol. 5 (1977), p. 43-49.

The Long-term Programme was signed in 1977 to run to 1990 and covers trade and cooperation in industry, energy and other fields. It is intended to 'assure the position of Finland and the Soviet Union at the top of the list in the qualitative development of economic relations between East and West'.

313 **Co-operation between Finland and the CMEA in 1973-1977.**
Ilkka Tapiola. *Yearbook of Finnish Foreign Policy*, vol. 5 (1977), p. 49-51.

A note of the work of the multilateral commission of Finland and the CMEA (Comecon) countries that was set up in 1973.

Finlandization

314 **The reality of "Finlandisation": living under the Soviet shadow.**
V. I. Punasalo. London: Institute for the Study of Conflict, 1978. 15p. (Conflict Studies, 93).

The pseudonymous author defines Finlandization as the increase of Soviet influence in Finland on all political as well as economic activity, and considers that Finlandization has been possible in Finland only because of the attitudes and actions of Finland's leaders. He concludes that Finlandization is a form of communist revolution without barricades.

315 **'Finlandization': a map to a metaphor.**
Adam M. Garfinkle. Philadelphia, Pennsylvania: Foreign Policy Research Institute, 1978. [vii] + 56p. (Monograph No. 24).

An essay about the Finlandization debate as it affects Europe, Finland's relations with the Soviet Union, and Soviet policy towards western Europe. Argues that Finland is particularly exposed to methodical pressure from the Soviet Union but that the countries of western Europe are not so exposed and any future Finlandization of them would be of their own making.

316 **Europe: the specter of Finlandization.**
Walter Laqueur. *Commentary*, vol. 64, no. 6 (Dec. 1977), p. 37-41.

Laqueur analyses the concept of Finlandization and examines it in a wider European context. He believes that Finland provides the USSR with a model for relations with its neighbours and that the model might be extended into western Europe. This article, with additional comments, is also published in Laqueur's *The political psychology of appeasement: Finlandization and other unpopular essays* (New Brunswick, New Jersey; London: Transaction Books, 1980, p. 3-22).

317 **From Helsinki to Moscow.**
Melvin J. Lasky. *Encounter*, vol. LIII, no. 2 (Aug. 1979), p. 82-92.

The article has three interesting pages on Finland, expressing typical uninformed surprise about the country's Western character but commenting shrewdly, in the context of Finlandization, that the Finns tend to consider their domestic situation vis-à-vis the USSR as a half-full not a half-empty bottle.

318 **Has Finland been Finlandised?**
George Maude. In: *Soviet foreign policy toward western Europe.* Edited by George Ginsburgs and Alvin Z. Rubinstein. New York; London: Praeger, 1978, p. 43-65.

Maude argues that Finland's position vis-à-vis the USSR is unique because of the Treaty of Friendship, Cooperation and Mutual Assistance; Finland does not therefore serve as an example illustrating the general character of Finlandization.

319 **Scandinavia and "Finlandization".**
H. Peter Krosby. *Scandinavian Review*, vol. 63, no. 2 (June 1975), p. 11-19.

The writer argues that there is no evidence that the Sovietization of Finland has ever been a goal of Soviet policy and that the actual situation of Finland fits none of the definitions of 'Finlandization'.

320 **The myth of "Finlandization".**
Erkki Mäentakanen. *Yearbook of Finnish Foreign Policy*, vol. 2 (1974), p. 34-39.

Not surprisingly, this article by a Finnish diplomat claims that the term 'Finlandization' is neither meaningful, descriptive nor analytically useful in the analysis of European politics.

Finland and détente: self-interest politics and Western reactions.
See item no. 297.

Economy, Finance and Banking

Economy

321 **OECD economic surveys: Finland (December 1979).**
Paris: OECD, 1979. 79p.

A valuable survey of the Finnish economy, regularly published by the Organisation for Economic Cooperation and Development. This survey reviews recent developments, the balance of payments, management policies, energy supply, and short-term prospects.

322 **Finland: a design for living. A survey.**
The Economist, vol. 272, no. 7100 (29 Sept. 1979). 28p.

A shrewd and informative survey of Finland's economy (with particular emphasis on energy), trade, relationships with the Soviet Union and the EEC, and current and future political problems.

323 **Finland 1990: economic prospects.**
Helsinki: Economic Planning Centre, 1977. 64p.

A shortened version of a Finnish report published in February 1977 and providing a long-term forecast of the Finnish economy. Covers the international environment and domestic resources, needs and the pattern of expenditure, production, distribution of income and finance, and 'the slow growth alternative'.

324 **Finland: a growing economy.**
Jussi Linnamo. Helsinki: Ministry for Foreign Affairs, 1967. [iv]+98p. (Reference Publications, 1).

Contains a lot of useful background information on the Finnish economy although the once-topical data is out of date.

325 **Economic survey: supplement to the budget proposal. Submitted by the government to parliament.**
Economics Department, Ministry of Finance. Helsinki: Valtion Painatuskeskus, 1949- . annual.

An important survey of economic developments, trade, production, consumption, financing, etc. Appendices provide a diary of economic events during the preceding two years and also statistical tables.

326 **National budget for Finland.**
Helsinki: Ministry of Finance Economic Department, 1960- . annual.

An important annual describing the economic forecasts in the budget, following the same pattern as the *Economic survey* (preceding item), together with a section of supplementary statistics.

327 **Quarterly Economic Review of Finland.**
London: The Economist Intelligence Unit, 1953- . quarterly.

Analyses current trends in the Finnish economy, providing a number of economic indicators as well as brief political news. An annual supplement provides basic economic information.

328 **FER: Finnish Economic Report.**
Helsinki: Information Agency for International Commerce, 1978- . monthly.

A periodical concentrating on economic and industrial news and trends.

329 **Nordic Economic Outlook.**
Stockholm: Swedish Industrial Publications, 1975- . semi-annual.

A publication providing brief but convenient surveys of the economies of each of the five Nordic countries and embodying forecasts of future prospects.

Bank of Finland Monthly Bulletin.
See item no. 333.

Economic Review.
See item no. 335.

Unitas.
See item no. 336.

Finland: sources of information. A selective list of publications 1960-1977.
See item no. 760.

Regional policy and development

330 **Finnish regional development policies.**
Erkki Laatto. *Bank of Finland Monthly Bulletin*, vol. 49, no. 10 (Oct. 1975), p. 20-23.

Describes the general aims of regional policy and explains how parts of the country are divided into zones and extra subsidy regions.

331 **New aims and means for Finnish regional policy.**
Erkki Laatto. *Bank of Finland Monthly Bulletin*, vol. 50, no. 12 (Dec. 1976), p. 20-24.

Follows the preceding article by explaining more recent legislation and planning.

Finance, banking and insurance

332 **Financial markets in Finland: a series of articles which appeared in the *Bank of Finland Monthly Bulletin* in 1970-1972. Revised in 1978.**
Helsinki: Bank of Finland, 1978. 63p.

The articles are: the Finnish financial markets, the Bank of Finland, monetary policy in Finland, bank inspection in Finland, the Finnish commercial banks, the Finnish savings banks, the Finnish cooperative banks, Postipankki (formerly the Post Office Savings Bank) in Finland, the Finnish insurance companies, Finnish mortgage credit institutions, Finnish development credit institutions, and the Helsinki Stock Exchange. A most convenient compilation.

333 **Bank of Finland Monthly Bulletin.**
Helsinki: Bank of Finland, 1921- . monthly.

Publishes regular statistics, surveys of the economy, authoritative specialized articles and news items. Among the regular articles are: 'Public finance in 19--' (Published in no. 6 of the following year), 'The balance of payments and foreign exchange policy in 19--' (in no. 4) and 'The Finnish economy in 19-- and the current outlook' (in no. 5). An index has been published: *Articles published in the Bank of Finland Monthly Bulletin 1921-1977* (Helsinki: Bank of Finland, 1978. 51p.). This comprises a classified index (by UDC), and subject and author indexes.

334 **Bank of Finland Year Book.**
Helsinki: Bank of Finland, 1921-

Covers economic developments for the year reviewed, central bank policy, the balance sheet and the income statement of the Bank of Finland, and the Bank of Finland and international organizations. Includes tables illustrating the activities of the bank.

335 **Economic Review.**

Helsinki: Kansallis-Osake-Pankki, 1948- . semi-annual.

Published by one of the large commercial banks, this periodical contains regular articles (with statistics) on the economic situation and economic development in Finland as well as other articles on various economic topics. There is an author index to articles published 1948-76 in no. 4, 1976, p. 17-22.

336 **Unitas.**

Helsinki: Union Bank of Finland, 1929- . quarterly.

Published by one of the large commercial banks, *Unitas* contains regular articles on the economic situation in Finland and on Finland's foreign assets and liabilities as well as other articles and statistics.

337 **The banking system of Finland.**

Helsinki: Finnish Bankers' Association, 1979. 2nd ed. 36p.

A brief outline of the Finnish banking system and financial markets. Includes some statistics and an appendix listing the commercial banks, savings banks, cooperative banks, insurance companies, and credit institutions of various kinds.

338 **Helsinki Stock Exchange 60 years.**

Raimo Ilaskivi. *Economic Review*, no. 2 (1972), p. 69-76.

A commemorative article which looks at the history of the Helsinki Stock Exchange, its turnover, number of listed companies and their shareholders.

339 **The development of public finance during the 1970s.**

Timo Relander. *Unitas*, vol. 52, no. 2 (1980), p. 59-69.

Examines the increase in public demand during the 1970s and the reason for it, deals with the development of state expenditure and state indebtedness, and considers the role of public finance during the 1980s.

340 **The development of the Finnish credit market in 1950-1978.**

Erkki Pihkala. *Unitas*, vol. 51, no. 2 (1979), p. 71-84.

Looks particularly at the role of the central bank (the Bank of Finland) and the growth of new credit sources.

341 **Inflation: causes and cures.**

Seppo Leppänen. Helsinki: Economic Planning Centre, 1980. [vii]+56p. bibliog.

A survey of inflation in Finland during the period 1960-79 by a senior official of the Economic Planning Centre, a government department subordinate to the Ministry of Finance.

342 **Monetary policy.**
T. R. G. Bingham, Antti Heinonen. *Bank of Finland Monthly Bulletin*, vol. 54, no. 7 (July 1980), p. 24-29.

Describes the successive periods of monetary stringency and ease through which the Finnish economy passed in the latter part of the 1970s and shows how Finnish monetary policy operates by influencing bank profitability.

343 **Finnish interest rates: structure, policy and developments, 1960-1978.**
Ralf Pauli, Olavi Rantala. *Bank of Finland Monthly Bulletin*, vol. 52, no. 12 (Dec. 1978), p. 20-26.

Interest rate policy has from time to time supplemented credit rationing as the basis for Finnish monetary policy.

344 **Finland's foreign debt - a structural weakness or unsound taxation.**
Kari Puumanen. *Economic Review*, no. 1 (1976), p. 17-29.

The author argues that the balance of payments problem is not based on structural weaknesses in the Finnish economy and on rapid industrialization but that the tax system encourages deficit spending and increases indebtedness. Another view is put in the following item.

345 **Debt-ridden Finland - but why?**
Henri J. Vartiainen. *Economic Review*, no. 2 (1976), p. 6-19.

A reply to the preceding item which stresses the expansion of the public sector and higher taxation as factors in explaining the deficit on the current account.

346 **Capital import policy in Finland.**
Peter Nyberg. *Bank of Finland Monthly Bulletin*, vol. 52, no. 11 (Nov. 1978), p. 20-23.

Describes how the Bank of Finland influences the volume and characteristics of capital imports. Gives figures for capital imports and the cost of the foreign debt.

347 **Price regulation in Finland 1968-1976.**
Timo Tyrväinen, Ilmo Pyyhtiä. *Bank of Finland Monthly Bulletin*, vol. 50, no. 8 (Aug. 1976), p. 20-26.

Looks at the inflationary bias of the Finnish economy and the role of price control legislation in restraining price expectations and contributing to bringing domestic price rises closer to the average international rate of inflation.

348 **The structure and development of service sector investment in Finland in 1953-1977.**
Jarmo Pesola, Timo Tyrväinen. *Bank of Finland Monthly Bulletin*, vol. 52, no. 3 (March 1978), p. 20-25.

The service sector is the major investor in the Finnish economy.

349 **Payment arrangements between Finland and the socialist countries.**
Inkeri Hirvensalo, Terhi Kivilahti. *Bank of Finland Monthly Bulletin*, vol. 51, no. 11 (Nov. 1977), p. 20-31.
Lists and describes Finland's clearing payment arrangements with the communist countries, details the balance of trade and payments between Finland and those countries in 1961-76, and concludes with a description of proposals for the abolition of the clearing payments system.

350 **Insurance in Finland.**
Helsinki: Finnish Insurance Information Centre, 1960-
Contains articles on different aspects of insurance, e.g. pensions, travel insurance. There are also some news items.

351 **Insurance in the national economy.**
Pekka Lahikainen. *Unitas*, vol. 48, no. 3 (1976), p. 139-49.
Examines insurance activity in Finland, the insurance companies' investments, their risk-bearing capacity and taxation.

Taxation

352 **Taxation in Finland: three articles which appeared in the *Bank of Finland Monthly Bulletin* in 1978.**
Lasse Aarnio. Helsinki: Bank of Finland, 1978. 24p.
The three articles in question, by Lasse Aarnio, are: 'Developments in Finnish taxation'; 'Direct taxation'; 'Indirect taxes and social security contributions'. They provide a detailed description of Finnish taxes and summarize the main features of taxation policy.

Cooperative movement

353 **The cooperative movement in Finland 1945-1974.**
Vesa Laakkonen. Helsinki: University of Helsinki, Department of Cooperative Research, 1977. 180p. bibliog. (Publications, 6).
Examines the activity of different cooperative organizations in Finland - involving all primary cooperatives from consumer cooperatives to cooperative slaughterhouses - against the background of the national economy. Extensive statistical information.

354 **The cooperative movement in Finland.**
Matti Kujala. Helsinki: University of Helsinki, 1975. 55p.

An informative short account of the history of the Finnish cooperative movement, the significant role of that movement in Finnish economic life, and the composition and administration of the various cooperatives - agricultural, wholesale, retail and banking. Includes statistics.

355 **The co-operative movement in Finland.**
Vesa Laakkonen. *Bank of Finland Monthly Bulletin*, vol. 50, no. 3 (March 1976), p. 20-27.

An examination of the number of cooperatives, their turnover, cooperative shops, cooperative processing and marketing of agricultural and forestry products, cooperative banks, and the role of cooperatives in the Finnish economy.

Trade, Industry and Transport

Foreign trade

356 **Finland's export experience: a survey of policies, institutions and methods.**
Geneva: International Trade Centre, United Nations Conference on Trade and Development, General Agreement on Tariffs and Trade, 1973. iv+300p. maps. (Export Promotion Handbooks).

A mine of information about the organization of Finnish foreign trade, discussing *inter alia* the government departments concerned, the Finnish Foreign Trade Association, the chambers of commerce, and business and language education. The summary (p. 256-61) lists the factors that have contributed to Finland's success as an exporter, and Finnish policies and measures are held up as an example to developing countries.

357 **Register of exporters.**
Helsinki: Finnish Foreign Trade Association, 1979. 334p.

The register offers information about a large number of Finnish companies for those seeking Finnish exporters of goods or services. Its principal language is English. There is an alphabetical list of goods and services, a classified list of exporters, and an alphabetical list of companies. The register is regularly revised.

358 **Finnish Trade Review.**
Helsinki: Finnish Foreign Trade Association, 1930- . 8 times per year.

Contains feature articles and news items relating to trade. Issues are thematic and addresses of manufacturers are always given for the promotion of trade.

359 **Finnfacts.**
Helsinki: Finnfacts Institute, [196-?] -. bimonthly.
A newsletter giving primarily economic and industrial news and news briefs, mostly relating to trade.

360 **Finland as a trading partner.**
Finnfacts Institute. Helsinki: Finnish Foreign Trade Association, 1980. rev. ed. 89p. map. bibliog.
'A concise guide to the Finnish industry and market...containing general information for both importers from and exporters to Finland.' Gives information on various industries with practical hints for the business traveller.

361 **Customs procedures in Finland.**
Helsinki: Board of Customs, 1975. 68p.
Translated from a text used for courses organized by the Finnish customs for customs officials from developing countries. Describes the general principles involved in the clearance of goods through Finnish customs, and includes examples of the types of forms used.

362 **Setting up in Finland.**
Helsinki: Commission for Foreign Investments, Ministry of Trade and Industry, 1980. [v]+23p.
This describes how to start a business in Finland, taking into account the changes brought about by the new legislation relating to foreign companies that came into effect in January 1980.

Hints to business men: Finland.
See item no. 93.

Industry

363 **Finnish industry 1980.**
Helsinki: Bureau for Economic Information, Finnfacts Institute, 1980. 36p.
Brief but central information on Finnish industries and the Finnish economy.

364 **Mistä mitäkin saa. Vem levererar vad i Finland. Who supplies what in Finland. VII. 1978.**
Helsinki: Sininen Kirja, 1977. [xiv]+440+[viii]+236p.
Contains three sections: alphabetical list of products, services and performances; name, address, telephone and telex of reported companies listed productwise; the most important companies in Finland listed branchwise. Arranged for use by readers of Finnish, Swedish and English.

365 **Sininen kirja XIV. [1979]. Tietoa yrityksistä yrityksille jo 50 vuoden ajan.** (Blue book XIV. Information about firms for firms for over 50 years.)
Helsinki: Sininen Kirja, 1978. [various]p.

This is an extensive directory of economic life in Finland. An alphabetical general index of firms leads to the main index of firms arranged by localities. Also includes a classified index of trades, information about government departments, municipal and other public bodies and establishments, a list of post offices and railway stations, and marketing information. English is one of several languages in which clear directions are given for use of the work.

366 **Suomen 2000 suurinta yritystä. Finlands 2000 största företag. The 2000 largest companies in Finland. Suomen talouselämän vuosikirja. Årsbok för Finlands näringsliv. Year-book of business in Finland.**
Helsinki: Yritystieto, 1972- . annual.

Originally published in 1972-75 as *Suomen 1500 suurinta yritystä* (The 1500 largest companies in Finland). Lists companies according to type of activity: industrial, trading, banks, etc. Information on type of activity, sales, exports, employees, capital, profit, etc. Alphabetical index.

367 **State owned companies in Finland.**
Helsinki: State Owned Companies Advisory Board, 1971- . annual.

An annually published description of the operations during the previous year of fourteen major and three smaller state-owned companies, giving information on turnover, staff, operations and financing, as well as balance sheets and income statements, etc. Subsidiaries of the companies are listed.

368 **Finnish industry in 1960-1985.**
Jarmo Pesola, Ilmo Pyyhtiä. *Bank of Finland Monthly Bulletin*, vol. 50, no. 1 (Jan. 1976), p. 20-25.

Looks at demand and investment, and the future prospects, with the Industrial Commission's estimates for 1975-85.

369 **Finnish industry: an overview.**
Jyrki Malmio, Heikki Tulokas. *Bank of Finland Monthly Bulletin*, vol. 51, no. 1 (Jan. 1977), p. 20-30.

About the structure of Finnish industry (categories and ownership), its production inputs (costs, raw materials and energy), financial structure, markets and future prospects. Argues for increased investment to improve productivity, to attain higher wages and discourage emigration.

370 **Small and medium-sized industrial firms in Finland.**
Heikki J. Kunnas. *Bank of Finland Monthly Bulletin*, vol. 53, no. 7 (July 1979), p. 24-29.

Describes the results of a study by SITRA, the Finnish National Fund for Research and Development. Shows that although small and medium-sized firms have become more capital-intensive, the capital invested per new vacancy is less than in large firms. Moreover, the value of output per employee is lower than in large firms.

371 **The Confederation of Finnish Industries.**
Timo Laatunen. *Economic Review*, no. 1 (1976), p. 3-9.

The Confederation of Finnish Industries (TKL) began activity in 1976. This article describes its origin, aims and organization, and lists its member associations.

372 **The Finnish metal and engineering industry.**
Erik Forsman, Martti Mäki. *Bank of Finland Monthly Bulletin*, vol. 51, no. 7 (July 1977), p. 20-25.

Deals with mineral resources, production, growth prospects, and exports.

373 **Finnish chemical industries and the building materials industry: an overview.**
Pertti Lehtiö, Kari Jalas, Veijo Heikkilä. *Bank of Finland Monthly Bulletin*, vol. 51, no. 12 (Dec. 1977), p. 20-25.

Considers separately the chemical industries and the building materials industry; examines particularly production and future prospects.

374 **Mining and quarrying in Finland.**
Urpo J. Salo. *Bank of Finland Monthly Bulletin*, vol. 49, no. 7 (July 1975), p. 20-29. map.

Examines, in broad outline, the development of geological research and prospecting, the country's mineral resources and the mining industry. Also reviews briefly the stone industry, the extraction of clay and gravel, and the peat industry. The map shows mines in operation, research projects and metallurgical factories. Charts show the output of different minerals.

375 **The Finnish Timber and Paper Calendar.**
Helsinki: Finnish Paper and Timber Journal, 1926- . biennial.

Sections on roundwood, sawmills, prefabricated timber houses, joinery and impregnated wood products, wood-based panels products, pulp, paper and board. There is a section of general information and there are indexes to firms, persons, agents and advertisers.

376 **Finnish Paper and Timber: Information Journal of the Finnish Forest Industry.**
Helsinki: Finnish Paper and Timber Journal, 1950- . bimonthly.

Information on the Finnish forest industry in the form of feature articles, statistics and news items.

377 **Finnish consumer goods industries: an overview.**
Bank of Finland Monthly Bulletin, vol. 51, no. 9 (Sept. 1977), p. 20-25.

Examines the manufacture of food, beverages and tobacco, the clothing industry, footware, leather, fur and similar products, and comments that these industries are faced with increasingly keen international competition.

378 **Recent trends in Finnish wholesale and retail trade.**
Matti Aura. *Bank of Finland Monthly Bulletin*, vol. 54, no. 8 (Aug. 1980), p. 1-2, 32.

Explains briefly the structure of wholesale and retail trade in Finland, notes the decline in the number of small shops, and suggests that the expected increase in the use of credit cards will contribute to a reduction in trading costs.

379 **Major boundary projects in the construction sector.**
Kauko Rastas. *Economic Review*, no. 2 (1978), p. 3-10.

An authoritative account of Finnish construction projects in the Soviet Union at Pääjärvi, Svetogorsk and Kostamus, projects which were due to peak in 1979. These building projects, situated near the Finnish frontier, are a valuable means of offsetting payments for Soviet oil.

380 **Joint Finnish-Soviet construction projects: their prospects and effects on trade.**
Hannu T. Linnainmaa. *Yearbook of Finnish Foreign Policy*, vol. 2 (1974), p. 14-19.

Looks at Soviet construction projects in Finland (nuclear power stations, a gas pipeline), as well as Finnish projects in the USSR, against the theoretical background of economic cooperation between capitalist and CMEA countries.

Energy

381 **Features of the Finnish energy economy.**
Helsinki: Ministry of Trade and Industry, Energy Department, 1978. [i]+25p.

On energy requirements, primary energy supply, and energy conservation.

382 **The Finnish energy policy programme: approved by the Council of State on 15th March 1979.**
Helsinki: Valtion Painatuskeskus, 1979. [v]+31p.

The energy policy adopted in 1979 is based on energy conservation and on increasing indigenous energy supplies, particularly of wood and peat. The resulting energy programme is due to be revised completely during the period to 1982.

383 **Guidelines for the Finnish energy policy in 1976-1985: a statement by the Finnish Energy Policy Commission.**
Helsinki: Ministry of Trade and Industry, 1977. [iii]+18f. (Committee Report 1976: 92).

The statement is based on a study (in Finnish only) of how Finnish energy consumption was going to develop to 1985. Forecasts are incorporated in various tables and graphs.

384 **Peat to ease the energy deficit.**
Lasse Nevanlinna, Harry Viheriävaara. *Look at Finland*, no. 4 (1974), p. 48-53.

Describes how Finland is increasing its production and consumption of peat and the significance of peat in the country's energy supply. The same article, unillustrated, appears in *Economic Review*, no. 1 (1974), p. 15-17.

385 **District heating and energy conservation.**
Gunnar Smeds. *Finnish Trade Review*, no. 1 (1979), p. 10-13.

District heating, i.e. the concentration of heating in large plants, is well developed in Finland. This article describes the development of district heating, the systems used, and the environmental benefits.

Transport and communications

386 **Transport and communications in Finland in the 1960s and 1970s.**
Antero Aarvala. *Bank of Finland Monthly Bulletin*, vol. 49, no. 11 (Nov. 1975), p. 20-25.

Examines the development of transport (passenger and freight) and communications (postal, telephone, telex and telegram traffic), covering volume, structure and investment.

387 **Suomen kulkuneuvot. Finlands kommunikationer.** (Finnish Transport.)
Helsinki: Suomen matkailuliitto, 1930- . quarterly.

Published by the Finnish Travel Association, this is the complete timetable of transport in Finland: trains, buses (except local city transport), air, sea and lake vessels. Known popularly by the name of its precursor, *Turisti* (1891-1930), the timetable includes directions for use and notes in English, German, French and Russian as well as Finnish and Swedish.

Shipping and waterways

388 **Finland in shipping and shipbuilding.**
Jorma Pohjanpalo. Helsinki: Ministry for Foreign Affairs, Press and Cultural Centre, 1978. 40p. map.

A handy summary, with pleasing illustrations, of the history of Finnish merchant shipping, and an account of its recovery and development since the losses of the Second World War and the armistice of 1944. It notes particularly the development of car ferry traffic, the importance of icebreakers, and the state of the shipbuilding industry.

389 **Finnish merchant shipping.**
Heikki Päivike. *Bank of Finland Monthly Bulletin*, vol. 53, no. 8 (Aug. 1979), p. 24-27.

Describes the age and structure of the Finnish merchant fleet, its objectives, receipts and profitability, employment and ownership.

390 **Icebreakers.**
Jorma Pohjanpalo. *Look at Finland*, no. 5 (1977), p. 26-29.

A short but authoritative article on the development of icebreakers in Finland, and a description of the vessels now in service. The icebreakers have permitted a significant reduction in seasonal fluctuations in seaborne trade.

391 **Icebreakers and winter shipping.**
Jorma Pohjanpalo. *Unitas*, vol. 50, no. 2 (1978), p. 71-79.

An important article about the development of Finnish icebreakers, with a table showing the details of the fleet between 1890 and 1976. Gives information about operating costs and the role of icebreakers and ice-strengthened ships in keeping shipping traffic moving in the winter.

392 **The friendship route.**
W. R. Mead. *Geographical Magazine* (London), vol. XLIX, no. 1 (Oct. 1976), p. 42, 45-46.

This article describes the building and post-war rebuilding of the Saimaa Canal, which links the Saimaa lake system of eastern Finland with the once Finnish and now Soviet port of Vyborg. The canal is of doubtful value now as an investment but its visual interest is considerable.

393 **Suomen valtameripurjehtijat. Finlands djupvattenseglare. The Finnish deep-water sailers.**
Edited by Markku Haapio, Altti Holmroos. Lieto, Finland: Etelä-Suomen Kustannus, 1979. 224p.

A short history of Finnish sailing vessels from coastal to ocean-going craft. There are descriptions of 131 vessels with numerous photographs from the collection of Captain Sten Lille. Titles and text are in Finnish, Swedish and English.

394 **The last tall ships: Gustaf Erikson and the Åland sailing fleets 1872-1947.**
Georg Kåhre, edited and with an introductory chapter by Basil Greenhill. Greenwich, England: Conway Maritime Press, 1978. 208p. map. bibliog.

This book, translated from the Swedish original edition of 1948 by Louis Mackay and with a few editorial changes, chronicles the life and times of Gustaf Erikson, the famous Mariehamn shipowner, and the sailing fleets of the Åland Islands in the period 1872-1947. The magnificent illustrations have been selected by the editor, who is Director of the National Maritime Museum. Appendix I lists the sailing vessels in Erikson's fleet and appendix II is a list of books for further reading.

395 **Mother sea.**
Elis Karlsson. London: Oxford University Press, 1964. xiii+264p.

An Åland sailor's often exciting experiences of sailing in the tall ships of his islands between the two world wars, preceded by an account of his childhood on Vårdö.

396 **The last grain race.**
Eric Newby. London: Hart-Davis, 1968. x+244p. (The Mariners Library, 48).

An exciting account of sailing in one of Erikson's barques, *Moshulu*, in the last grain race from Australia in 1939, and of the sailors of the crew.

Railways

397 **Eisenbahnen in Finnland.** (Railways in Finland.)
Mikko Alameri. Vienna: Otto Slezak, 1979. 192p. maps. bibliog.

On the history and present state of railways in Finland, their motive power and rolling stock. Numerous illustrations and diagrams of locomotives and rolling stock.

398 **Masterpieces in steam.**
Colin D. Garratt. London: Blandford, 1973. 204p. maps. (Last Steam Locomotives of the World).

Finland, p. 134-56. A good description of the steam locomotives surviving at the time of writing with several illustrations of Finnish locomotives.

399 **Steam locomotives of Finland.**
London: Union Publications, 1966. 40p.

A list of locomotives of the Finnish State Railways and of private and industrial lines. Gives number, wheel arrangement, maker and date. Sixteen illustrations.

Air travel

400 **Finnair 1923-1973.**

Helsinki: Finnair, 1973. 87p.

A short jubilee history of Finland's national airline, also containing some background about Finnish aviation in general. Information is provided about the main aircraft types employed and there are some operating statistics for the period 1924-72.

Agriculture and Forestry

Agriculture

401 **Agricultural policy in Finland.**
Paris: Organisation for Economic Cooperation and Development, 1975. 51p. map. (Agricultural Policy Reports).

Divided into two sections: I 'The state of agriculture', and II 'Policy objectives and measures'. A thorough, concise and clearly presented account of its subject, with numerous statistical tables.

402 **Finnish farming: typology and economics.**
Uuno Varjo. Budapest: Akadémiai Kiadó, 1977. 146p. maps. bibliog. (Geography of World Agriculture, 6).

An important study of farming in Finland, dealing with the natural conditions, settlement, mechanization, land ownership and utilization, arable farming, animal husbandry, forestry on the farm, and the basic farm production types and farming regions.

403 **Farming in Finland.**
W. R. Mead. London: Athlone Press, 1953. [xv]+248p. maps.

'A descriptive study of the geography of Finnish farming.' Shows how land has been won for cultivation, describes the exploitation of the forest, grassland and crop husbandry, and looks at the land ownership pattern. The problems involved in the resettlement of refugees after the wars of 1939-40 and 1941-44 are carefully described. This book has not been displaced as an account of Finnish farming of the 1940s and early 1950s.

404 **Finnish agriculture.**
Nils Westermarck. Helsinki: Kirjayhtymä, 1969. 4th ed. 83p. maps. bibliog.

Now dated, but some useful information may still be obtained, for example about the effects of the Finnish climate on agriculture.

405 **The outlook for Finnish agriculture in the 1980s.**
Samuli Suomela. *Bank of Finland Monthly Bulletin*, vol. 54, no. 8 (Aug. 1980), p. 24-28.

Not simply a look at the future but also a survey of the 1970s. The author is Director-General of the National Board of Agriculture.

406 **Developments in the structure of Finnish agriculture in 1960-1975.**
Samuli Suomela. *Bank of Finland Monthly Bulletin*, vol. 49, no. 12 (Dec. 1975), p. 20-23.

The developments described here are the decline in the number of small farms, the small increase in the size of the average farm, and the legislation designed to increase farm size and to reduce surplus production by taking farms out of cultivation.

407 **Dairy farming in Finland: geographical aspects of the development, typology and economics of Finnish dairy farming.**
Paavo Talman. Oulu, Finland: Department of Geography, University of Oulu, 1978. 143p. maps. bibliog. (Publicationes Instituti Geographici Universitatis Ouluensis, 62).

'The work aims to describe the areal differentiation of dairy farming in Finland by reference to its structure, developmental features, role within agriculture, and profitability and the factors involved in this, and to construct a regional typology on the basis of these results.' Dairying is the most important branch of production within Finnish farming.

408 **Reindeer husbandry in Finland.**
Reijo K. Helle. *Geographical Journal*, vol. 145, pt. 2 (July 1979), p. 254-64. maps.

'To a growing extent reindeer husbandry in Finland occurs side by side with modern industrial and urban society. The reindeer economy has been on the losing side. However, because of the amount of work invested in the reindeer, the number of these animals is larger than before. It seems clear that the number of reindeer is at its maximum, as there is no longer excess capacity of lichen land for reindeer to graze in winter.'

409 **The modernisation of Finnish peasant farming in the late nineteenth and early twentieth centuries.**
Veikko Anttila. *Scandinavian Economic History Review*, vol. XXIV, no. 1 (1976), p. 33-44.

This article is concerned with the social and economic geography of the modernization of Finnish agriculture. It is based on an ethnological study, and is by an ethnologist.

Forestry

410 **Yearbook of Forest Industries.**
Helsinki: Central Association of Finnish Forest Industries, 1980. 40p.

Reviews the development of the Finnish forest industry in the previous year, provides statistics on production and exports, and gives information about the Central Association of Finnish Forest Industries and its member companies.

411 **Forest resources, forest ownership and their development in Finland.**
Kullervo Kuusela. *Bank of Finland Monthly Bulletin*, vol. 53, no. 1 (Jan. 1979), p. 20-28.

Based on the national forest inventories carried out by the Forest Research Institute. 'The forest balance indicates the accrual of mature timber crop in the forests.'

412 **Additional raw material for the forest industry by intensified recovery of wood.**
Pentti Hakkila. *Economic Review*, no. 2 (1975), p. 11-21.

Describes the use of forest residues as a raw material reserve as well as the possible utilization of whole small-sized trees.

The Finnish Timber and Paper Calendar.
See item no. 375.

Finnish Paper and Timber: Information Journal of the Finnish Forest Industry.
See item no. 376.

Employment and Labour

413 **Manpower policy in Finland.**
Paris: Organisation for Economic Cooperation and Development, 1977. 155p. maps. (OECD Reviews of Manpower and Social Policies, 17).

Explains and comments on Finnish manpower policy which is considered 'ingenious and inventive within given constraints'. Sections on specific policy problems: anti-cyclical policies, regional development policy, external migration, vocational rehabilitation and placement for the disadvantaged, a coordinated approach to education and employment, and interrelating the manpower policies of government and enterprises.

414 **Employment in Finland in the 1970s.**
Lauri Korpelainen. *Bank of Finland Monthly Bulletin*, vol. 53, no. 3 (March 1979), p. 24-31.

Examines developments in the Finnish labour market in terms of both supply and demand, covering the prevention of unemployment and the promotion of employment as well as discussions about the curbing of the supply of labour.

415 **New challenges for manpower policy.**
Lauri Korpelainen. *Unitas*, vol. 51, no. 4 (1979), p. 203-12.

Forecasts labour supply, the employment outlook and considers the problems posed by automation and unemployment and by reductions in working hours.

416 **The outlook for the supply of labour in Finland up to 2000.**
Pekka Parkkinen. *Bank of Finland Monthly Bulletin*, vol. 49, no. 1 (Jan. 1975), p. 20-24.

Examines population developments and developments in the supply of labour as well as prospects for balancing the supply and demand for labour.

417 **Labor in Finland.**
Carl Erik Knoellinger. Cambridge, Massachusetts: Harvard University Press, 1960. [xiv]+300p. map. (Wertheim Publications in Industrial Relations).

'Primarily concerns trends and problems in the Finnish labor market.' In fact this is a history of the development of Finnish trade unions, employers' organizations, labour legislation and collective bargaining up to 1958. Appendices give translations of the texts of various relevant agreements, laws and articles of association. No bibliography, but extensive references in the notes.

418 **SAK today.**
Helsinki: Central Organisation of Finnish Trade Unions SAK, 1976. 15p.

A brief, glossy pamphlet about the activities and aims of the Finnish trade unions. Includes a list of unions belonging to SAK (Suomen Ammattiliittojen Keskusjärjestö), the Central Organization of Finnish Trade Unions.

419 **Programme of principles of the Central Organisation of Finnish Trade Unions SAK adopted at the 10th General Congress of SAK 1971.**
Helsinki: Central Organisation of Finnish Trade Unions SAK, 1978. 15p.

A statement of what the trade union movement in Finland is aiming to do.

Statistics

420 **Guide to Finnish statistics 1977.**
Edited by Mauri Levomäki, Matti Kyrö. Helsinki: Tilastokeskus, 1977 [2]+51p. (Käsikirjoja. Handböcker. Handbooks, 8).

A guide to who compiles statistics in Finland and where they are published. There is a detailed list of contents but no index. The work is an abridged version of *Tilasto-opas 1975* (Guide to statistics 1975). Some of the titles of statistical series and publications and all the publishing bodies are given in English translation which complicates reference to the originals. Reference may be necessary to *Tilasto-opas 1978* (Guide to statistics 1978), (Helsinki: Tilastokeskus, 1978. 153p.) (Käsikirjoja [Handbooks], 3), the latest published.

421 **Finland in figures. 1979.**
Helsinki: Central Statistical Office, 1979. 32p.

An annually published, small-format 'instant dose of information' on Finland.

422 **Suomen tilastollinen vuosikirja. Statistisk årsbok för Finland. Statistical Yearbook of Finland.**
Helsinki: Tilastokeskus, 1878- . annual.

The *Statistical Yearbook of Finland* contains a wide selection of the most important statistical data on the country, and in recent years also information about other countries for comparative purposes. The yearbook was entitled *Suomenmaan tilastollinen vuosikirja. Annuaire Statistique pour la Finlande* (Statistical Yearbook of Finland) from 1879-1902, vols. 1-23. A new series began in 1903 which still continues, although with the issue for 1953 English displaced French as the foreign language used and the English title (Statistical Yearbook of Finland) was added to the Finnish and Swedish (Statistisk årsbok för Finland) titles. The texts and tables are thus now in Finnish, Swedish and English.

423 **Suomen virallinen tilasto.** (Official statistics of Finland.)
Helsinki: 1866-

This is the most important national statistical series, originally published in 1866-1904 with the title *Suomenmaan virallinen tilasto* (Official statistics of

Finland). There are several sub-series - at present over thirty produced by the Central Statistical Office (Tilastokeskus) and twelve by other national institutions. The main series are: IA, Foreign trade; IA, Foreign trade, monthly publication; IBa, Merchant fleet; IBb, Navigation; IB, Shipping between Finland and foreign countries; III, Agriculture; IVB, Statistics of income and property; VIA, Vital statistics; VIB, Causes of death; VIC, Population censuses; VII, Bank statistics; X, General education; XI, Public health and medical care; XIII, Post and Telegraph Office; XIV, Land surveying; XVIIA, Yearbook of forest statistics; XVIIIA, Industrial statistics; XVIIIC, House construction statistics; XVIIID, Production of dwellings; XIX, Public roads and waterways; XX, Railways; XXI, Social welfare and assistance; XXIIA, Insurance companies; XXIII, Judicial statistics; XXVIA, Accident statistics, industrial accidents; XXIX, Statistics of elections; XXXI, Communal finances; XXXII, Special social studies; XXXIV, Veterinary service; XXXV, General economic statistics; XXXVI, Yearbook of transport statistics; XXXVII, Higher education; XXXVIII, Research statistics; XXXIX, Farm economy; XL, Labour force survey.

424 **Elinolosuhteet 1950-1975. Levnadsförhållanden 1950-1975. Living conditions 1950-1975. Tilastotietoja suomalaisten elämisen laadusta ja siihen vaikuttavista tekijöistä. Statistiska uppgifter om finländarnas levnadskvalitet och faktorer som inverkar på denna. Statistical information on the quality of life in Finland and factors influencing it.**
Helsinki: Tilastokeskus, 1977. 228p. maps. (Tilastollisia tiedonantoja. Statistiska meddelanden. Statistical Surveys, 58).

An experimental volume of statistics describing living conditions in Finland. General introductory material and headings of tables in English as well as Finnish and Swedish. List of tables and figures; English vocabulary. Covers economic factors, population, conditions of work, distribution of income, health, education and research, social security, housing, environment, culture, information, leisure, social participation, judicial conditions and collective security, equality of regions and traffic conditions, equality of sexes and age-groups, equality of languages and ethnic groups. Good graphic presentation.

425 **Kulttuuritilasto. Kulturstatistik. Cultural statistics. 1977. Tilastotietoja taiteesta, tiedonvälityksestä, vapaa-ajasta, urheilusta ja nuoritoiminnasta vuosilta 1930-1977. Statistiska uppgifter om konst, massmedia, fritid, idrott och ungdomsverksamhet åren 1930-1977. Statistical information on arts, communication, leisure, sports and youth activities in 1930-1977.**
Helsinki: Tilastokeskus, 1978. 256p. (Tilastollisia tiedonantoja. Statistiska meddelanden. Statistical Surveys, 60).

An experimental volume, the coverage of which is defined in its title.

426 **Yearbook of Nordic Statistics. Nordisk statistisk årsbok.**
Stockholm: Nordic Council and the Nordic Statistical Secretariat, 1963- . annual.

From a modest beginning, this work has grown into an extensive publication providing data on Denmark, Finland, Iceland, Norway and Sweden, and including the Faroe Islands and Greenland, with a view to facilitating comparisons between the Nordic countries. The coverage includes population, agriculture, mining and manufacturing, trade, public finance and social statistics. The languages now used are English and Swedish, and from 1973 the volumes have subject indexes. The *Yearbook* is published in the series 'Nordisk udredningsserie' (Nordic Official Reports) as the last volume of each year, as follows: 1962 no. 10; 1963 no. 8; 1964 no. 10; 1965 no. 14; 1966 no. 10; 1967 no. 17; 1968 no. 19; 1969 no. 22; 1970 no. 23; 1971 no. 21; 1972 no. 12; 1973 no. 24; 1974 no. 29; 1975 no. 38; 1976 no. 35; 1977 no. A-18; 1978 no. A-18; 1979 no. A-26.

Väestönlaskenta. Folkräkningen. Population census. 1970.
See item no. 194.

Naisten asema. Kvinnornas ställning. Position of women.
See item no. 200.

Maassamuutto sekä Suomen ja Ruotsin välinen muuttoliike 1950-1975. Inrikes omflyttning samt omflyttning mellan Finland och Sverige 1950-1975. Internal migration and migration between Finland and Sweden in 1950-1975.
See item no. 218.

Education

General

427 **The science of education in Finland 1828-1918.**
Taimo Iisalo. Helsinki: Societas Scientiarum Fennica, 1979. 110p. bibliog. (The History of Learning and Science in Finland 1828-1918, 18).

A history of the aims and theories of education in Finland during the period 1828-1918.

428 **Education profile: Finland.**
Helsinki: British Council; London: Education Liaison Unit, British Council, 1978. [v]+29+3p. map. bibliog.

An extremely clear outline of the Finnish educational system, its administration, finance, development and planning. It is particularly helpful that the original Finnish terms for types of schools, examinations, etc. are given as well as English translations. An appendix provides basic educational statistics. The publication may be obtained from the British Council in London.

429 **Educational development in Finland 1976-1978: report by the Finnish Ministry of Education to the 37th Session of the International Conference on Education in Geneva, July 1979.**
Helsinki: Ministry of Education, 1979. 134p. (Reference Publications, 9).

A handy summary of the organization and structure of the education system in Finland (general and vocational education, higher education, teacher training and adult education).

Schools

430 **Going comprehensive.**
Jukka Sarjala. *Look at Finland*, no. 4 (1978), p. 54-57.
Finnish education is now comprehensive, following legislation in 1968. The aims, curriculum and character of Finnish comprehensive schools are described briefly and sympathetically in this article.

Higher education

431 **University of Helsinki: a short history.**
Matti Klinge. Helsinki: University of Helsinki, 1977. 2nd rev. ed. 48p.
Traces the history of the country's oldest university from its beginnings in Turku in 1640 to the present day.

432 **Higher education and research in Finland.**
Helsinki: Ministry of Education, 1973. 104p. (Reference Publication, 6).
Contents: I, Administration of higher education and research; II, Higher education; III, Research. Appendices list institutions of higher education (with the degrees and diplomas taught) and government research institutes, with their addresses. Brief but informative.

433 **Finnish university problems.**
CRE-information, n.s., no. 45 (1st quarter 1979), 82p.
The VIIth General Assembly of CRE, the Standing Conference of Rectors and Vice-Chancellors of the European Universities, met in Helsinki in August 1979, and this issue of the Conference's quarterly journal was devoted to Finnish university problems. It contains three articles in English and three in French (each with a summary in the other language) on such topics as reforms to the degree syllabus, research policy and university financing.

Other education

434 **Adult Education in Finland.**
Helsinki: Kansanvalistusseura (Society for Popular Culture), 1964- . quarterly.
'Aims to promote increased international contact in the field of adult education.' Publishes articles on various aspects of adult education in Finland, interpreted

very widely, and issues are frequently devoted to a particular theme (e.g. no. 3, 1979, on the family).

435 **Vocational education in Finland.**
Helsinki: National Board of Vocational Education, 1973. 154p. maps.

A description of the organization of vocational education, the types of institutions involved and the nature of the courses offered - from cosmetology to the breeding of fur-bearing animals.

Physical education and sports in Finland.
See item no. 685.

Learning, Science and Technology

Scholarship and the sciences

436 **Classical studies in Finland 1828-1918.**
Pentti Aalto. Helsinki: Societas Scientiarum Fennica, 1980. 210p. bibliog. (The History of Learning and Science in Finland 1828-1918, 10a).

Looks at Latin and Greek philology, ancient history, Roman law, ancient philosophy, fine arts, and New Testament philology and patristics. Has a final chapter on 'The contribution of Finland to classical scholarship'.

437 **Oriental studies in Finland 1828-1918.**
Pentti Aalto. Helsinki: Societas Scientiarum Fennica, 1971. 174p. map. bibliog. (The History of Learning and Science in Finland 1828-1918, 10b).

A concise and informative account of its subject, including much on exploration by Finns as well as on linguistic, literary, archaeological, ethnographical and anthropological studies.

438 **Contemporary philosophy in Scandinavia.**
Edited by Raymond E. Olson, Anthony M. Paul. Baltimore, Maryland; London: Johns Hopkins Press, 1972. [xi]+508p. bibliog.

The book consists of chapters by modern Scandinavian philosophers on topics in which they have specialized, grouped into three parts: I, Logic, philosophy of language, epistemology and the philosophy of science; II, Ethics, and political and legal philosophy; III, Philosophy of history, and historical and interpretive studies. Some of the chapters are by Finnish philosophers and the distinguished Finnish logician G. H. von Wright has contributed an introduction on the present situation in philosophy in Denmark, Finland, Norway and Sweden, set against the background of its evolution from the beginning of the 19th century.

439 **Finland: sociology in Finland.**
Erik Allardt. *Current Sociology. La Sociologie Contemporaine*, vol. 25, no. 1 (1977), p. 29-56.

This number of *Current Sociology* took the form of a 'Trend report' on Scandinavian sociology. Allardt, who is Professor of Sociology at the University of Helsinki, describes the traditions and history of sociology in Finland, the subject's institutional organization, and the types of sociological research and method pursued in contemporary Finland. The article includes a bibliography, 'Finnish Sociology', on p. 147-52.

440 **Sociology in Finland: notes on main traditions in sociology and on some of their exponents with an emphasis on the period since 1945.**
Heikki Leimu. *Zeitschrift für Soziologie*, vol. 6, no. 2 (April 1977), p. 222-49. bibliog.

Describes the main traditions in Finnish sociology: social anthropology and ethnology, concrete social studies, social psychology and general sociology with discussions of the work of sociologists in these areas; also considers the status of sociology and of institutes of sociology within teaching and research. There is an extensive list of references.

441 **The history of medicine in Finland 1828-1918.**
Bertel von Bonsdorff. Helsinki: Societas Scientiarum Fennica, 1975. 309p. map. bibliog. (The History of Learning and Science in Finland 1828-1918, 3).

Includes brief sections on dentistry and veterinary medicine.

442 **The medieval leper and his northern heirs.**
Peter Richards. Cambridge, England: D. S. Brewer; Totowa, New Jersey: Rowman & Littlefield, 1977. xvi+178p. maps. bibliog.

An account by a Professor of Medicine of how sufferers from leprosy were treated in Britain and northern Europe not only in the Middle Ages but also into the modern period, since the disease lingered in Scandinavia until a few years ago. The lepers of the Åland Islands in the 17th century are taken as an example of the conditions imposed on those who suffered from the disease. An unusual piece of medical and social history.

443 **The history of botany in Finland 1828-1918. With an appendix on forest science by Yrjö Ilvessalo.**
Runar Collander. Helsinki: Societas Scientiarum Fennica, 1965. 159p. bibliog. (The History of Learning and Science in Finland 1828-1918, 8).

One of the first volumes to be published in a distinguished series.

444 **The history of chemistry in Finland 1828-1918, with chapters on the political, economic and industrial background.**
Terje Enkvist. Helsinki: Societas Scientiarum Fennica, 1972. 161p. map. bibliog. (The History of Learning and Science in Finland 1828-1918, 6).

Includes pharmaceutical chemistry and chemical technology.

445 **The history of geology and mineralogy in Finland 1828-1918.**
Hans Hausen. Helsinki: Societas Scientiarum Fennica, 1968. 147p. bibliog. (The History of Learning and Science in Finland 1828-1918, 7a).

Covers the history of geology and mineralogy, the work of the Geological Commission and prospecting and mining enterprises.

446 **The history of geophysics in Finland 1828-1918.**
Heikki Simojoki. Helsinki: Societas Scientiarum Fennica, 1978. 157p. bibliog. (The History of Learning and Science in Finland 1828-1918, 5b).

On geophysics, meteorology, oceanography, hydrography, geomagnetism and seismology.

Archaeology in Finland before 1920.
See item no. 101.

Ethnology in Finland before 1920.
See item no. 105.

Scandinavian Political Studies: a Journal Published by the Nordic Political Science Association: Denmark, Finland, Iceland, Norway and Sweden.
See item no. 262.

The science of education in Finland 1828-1918.
See item no. 427.

Finnish folklore research 1828-1918.
See item no. 509.

A hundred years of Finnish folklore research: a reappraisal.
See item no. 510.

Scientific and industrial policy

447 **Governmental science policy in Finland: report on the Finnish science administration, finances and policies.**
Tarmo Lemola, Teuvo Räty, Esko Vesikansa. Helsinki: Academy of Finland, 1975. [vi]+73p.

A short survey of governmental science policy, the organization of research and the resources allocated for research, and of the direction and development of research. Based on an analysis of the state budgets for the preceding five years.

448 **SITRA's ten years of operation.**
Bank of Finland Monthly Bulletin, vol. 52, no. 5 (May 1978), p. 1-2, 28.

The Finnish National Fund for Research and Development (SITRA) was founded in 1967; the interest on its capital was intended to be used to promote the country's economic development. It has mainly provided finance for the promotion of new technology and innovations.

Languages

Finnish

449 **Finno-Ugrian languages and peoples.**
Péter Hajdú, translated and adapted by G. F. Cushing. London: Deutsch, 1975. 254p. maps. bibliog. (The Language Library).

Designed to describe the Finno-Ugrian peoples and languages to interested, but non-specialist, English-speaking readers. Sets the Finns and Finnish as well as the Lapps and Lapp into their Finno-Ugrian context.

450 **Survey of the Uralic languages.**
Compiled by Björn Collinder. Stockholm: Almqvist & Wiksell, 1957. xxii+539p.

This is a descriptive survey of the chief languages of the Uralic family. Finnish is covered on p. 1-131 and Lapp on p. 181-225. Finnish is treated particularly thoroughly with a good traditional approach and the grammar and texts (with lexical glosses) provided constitute a progressive elementary course enabling a linguistically capable reader to attain a good reading ability in Finnish.

451 **The structure and development of the Finnish language.**
Lauri Hakulinen. Bloomington, Indiana: Indiana University, 1961. ix+383p. (Indiana University Publications. Uralic and Altaic Series, 3).

Hakulinen's work is the standard account of its subject. The later editions which have appeared of the Finnish original, *Suomen kielen rakenne ja kehitys* (Helsinki: Otava, 1979. 4th ed., rev. and enl. 633p. bibliog.) (Otavan korkeakoulukirjasto [Otava's University Library]), have advanced beyond this reduced translation. It is strong on phonology, morphology and lexicology; sparse on grammar and syntax.

452 **The language barrier.**
Michael Branch. *Books from Finland*, vol. XIII, no. 2 (1979), p. 68-71.

Refers to the traditional view that Finnish is a difficult language, assesses various currently available textbooks, and notes the recent consolidation of Finnish teaching abroad with the help of Finnish lectors supported by the Ministry of Education.

453 **Finnish.**
J. E. O. Screen. In: *A guide to foreign language courses and dictionaries.* Edited by A. J. Walford and J. E. O. Screen. London: Library Association, 1977. 3rd rev. and enl. ed. p. 255-59.

A short and selective survey of published courses, grammars and dictionaries available at the time of compilation. Intended as a guide for teachers, students and librarians.

454 **Finnish.**
London: Centre for Information on Language Teaching and Research, 1975. 11f. (Language and Culture Guides, 8).

Contains details of taught courses, research in progress in Britain, a list of dictionaries, grammars and readers, and sources of further information. A revised edition is in preparation and due for publication in 1981.

455 **Suomen kielen ja Suomen kulttuurin opinnot kesällä 1980. Att studera finska och Finlands kultur sommaren 1980. Courses in Finnish language and culture summer 1980.**
Helsinki: Ministry of Education, Department of International Relations [and] Council for Instruction of Finnish for Foreigners, 1980. 61p.

Provides details of courses in Finland for the beginner and the more advanced student. Also lists teachers of Finnish language and culture outside Finland and textbooks. Annual.

456 **Finnish courses in Great Britain 1980/1981.**
London: Finnish Embassy and University of London, School of Slavonic and East European Studies, 1980. 7f.

An annually produced list of degree courses, of courses in which Finnish forms part of a degree, of evening courses and Saturday schools (the last principally for children). Addresses are given from which further details of the courses listed may be obtained. The list is available from the Finnish Embassy, 38, Chesham Place, London SW1X 8HW, or from the School of Slavonic and East European Studies, University of London, Senate House, London WC1E 7HU.

457 **Virittäjä: Kotikielen seuran aikakauslehti.** (Journal of the Society for the Mother Tongue.)
Helsinki: Kotikielen seura, 1883, 1886, 1897- . quarterly.

The most important periodical for the study of Finnish. Publishes articles, reviews, and a section on the use of Finnish. The articles have abstracts in English or German.

458 **Sananjalka: Suomen kielen seuran vuosikirja.** (Yearbook of the Finnish Language Society.)
Turku, Finland: Suomen kielen seura,1959- . annual.

An annual on the Finnish language and the linguistic aspects of literature and ethnography.

Dictionaries

459 **Suomalais-englantilainen suursanakirja. Finnish-English general dictionary.**
V. S. Alanne. Porvoo, Finland: Werner Söderström, 1979. 3rd ed. reprinted. XXV+1,111p.

The best large Finnish-English dictionary, with many examples of usage and some colloquialisms. Includes a number of features of value to the English-speaking user, e.g. the citation alongside the infinitive of the present tense first-person singular where this is irregular.

460 **Suomalais-englantilainen sanakirja.** (Finnish-English dictionary.)
P. E. Halme. Helsinki: Suomalaisen Kirjallisuuden Seura, 1973. 2nd ed. 632p. (Suomalaisen Kirjallisuuden Seuran toimituksia, Publications of the Society of Finnish Literature, 255).

A medium-sized Finnish-English dictionary. Gives the explanations of symbols and abbreviations in English as well as Finnish.

461 **Finnish-English dictionary. Suomalais-englantilainen koulusanakirja.**
Aino Wuolle. Porvoo, Finland: Werner Söderström, 1976. 11th ed. [viii]+485p.

462 **English-Finnish dictionary. Englantilais-suomalainen opiskelusanakirja.**
Aino Wuolle. Porvoo, Finland: Werner Söderström, 1979. 12th ed. [viii]+492p.

This volume and the preceding item are small dictionaries, significantly described as school or study dictionaries in their Finnish titles. They are in many ways adequate for the beginner who does not intend to advance very far.

463 **Englantilais-suomalainen suursanakirja. English-Finnish general dictionary.**
Raija Hurme, Maritta Pesonen. Porvoo, Finland: Werner Söderström, 1978. 2nd rev. and enl. ed. xi+1,183p.

The companion volume to Alanne's dictionary *Suomalais-englantilainen suursanakirja* (q.v.). This is the most extensive English-Finnish dictionary but is not worth more than that by Tuomikoski and Slöör (see the following item).

464 **Englantilais-suomalainen sanakirja.** (English-Finnish dictionary.)
Aune Tuomikoski, Anna Slöör. Helsinki: Suomalaisen Kirjallisuuden Seura, 1973. 6th ed. xiii+1,100p.

Much older in origin than the dictionary of Hurme and Pesonen (see the preceding item), but continues to be valuable because of its broad scope and good examples of usage. Remains the best value for money.

465 **Englantilais-suomalainen sanakirja.** (English-Finnish dictionary.)
Eeva Riikonen, Maija Tammelin, Sirkka Auli. Helsinki: Otava, 1979. 740p.

This is based on the 9th (1974) edition of the medium-sized dictionary by Eeva Riikonen and Aune Tuomikoski which was originally published in 1964. No concessions are made to possible English users either in how to use the dictionary or in explanations of the Finnish abbreviations. For most purposes the larger dictionaries by Hurme and Pesonen (q.v.) and Tuomikoski and Slöör (q.v.) remain preferable.

466 **Suomi-englanti-suomi taskusanakirja.**
(Finnish-English-Finnish pocket dictionary.)
Aino Wuolle. Porvoo, Finland: Werner Söderström, 1979. 4th ed. [vi]+200+191+78p.

The last section consists of a vocabulary and dialogues for a visit to London.

467 **Finnish for travellers.**
Lausanne, Switzerland: Berlitz, 1976. 192p.
Contains useful phrases and vocabularies. A cassette or record is advertised with the book.

468 **Englantilais-suomalainen idiomisanakirja. I osa: verbit. English-Finnish dictionary of idioms. Part one: verbal idioms.**
Kingsley Hart, Aarne T. K. Lahtinen. Helsinki: Otava, 1965. 340p.
This contains the Finnish equivalents of a good variety of English formal and informal verbal idioms. The index from Finnish to English (p. 333-40) makes it possible to find English equivalents of some Finnish verbal idioms.

469 **Englantilais-suomalainen tekniikan sanakirja.**
(English-Finnish technical dictionary.)
Anja Easterling, Toivo J. Koivula. Helsinki: Tammi, 1980. 2nd rev. ed. 301p.
A small dictionary which contains about 16,000 words.

470 **Englantilais-suomalainen tekniikan ja kaupan sanakirja.**
(English-Finnish technical and commercial dictionary.)
Jyrki K. Talvitie, Yrjö Talvitie, Ahti Hytönen. Helsinki: Tietoteos, 1979. 7th ed. 584p.
Contains about 160,000 entry words, a list of geographical names and a list of English abbreviations. Directions for the Finnish user only. A companion Finnish-English volume has been announced.

471 **Nykysuomen sanakirja. Lyhentämätön kansanpainos.**
(Dictionary of modern Finnish. Unabridged popular edition.)
Porvoo, Finland: Werner Söderström, 1978-80. 6th printing. 5 vols.
The standard dictionary of the Finnish language. Volumes 1-3 comprise the dictionary proper, volume 4 is a dictionary of foreign words in Finnish (vierasperäiset sanat), and volume 5 contains neologisms, slang, abbreviations and foreign place-names.

472 **A student's glossary of Finnish: the literary language arranged by frequency and alphabet. English-French-German-Hungarian-Russian-Swedish.**
Michael Branch, Antero Niemikorpi, Pauli Saukkonen. Porvoo, Finland: Werner Söderström. 1980. 378p.
This sturdily produced glossary contains 1,899 words, providing a vocabulary for a basic course in Finnish. The introductory sections discuss the applications of the glossary in the teaching of Finnish and give a brief report on the programming principles involved in the selection of the vocabulary. The glossary in order of frequency is followed by an alphabetical section which includes frequency codes,

enabling teachers to assess the level of difficulty of a text. The work can serve as a textbook for teacher and student and as a reference book for the student. It will be especially helpful for teaching students to read Finnish, the translations in six languages widening the opportunities of use. A set of paradigms is reproduced at the end of the book.

473 **Suomen kielen taajuussanasto. A frequency dictionary of Finnish.**
Pauli Saukkonen, Marjatta Haipus, Antero Niemikorpi, Helena Sulkala. Porvoo, Finland: Werner Söderström, 1979. 536p.

The first general frequency dictionary of Finnish, drawn from an analysis of over 400,000 word occurrences collected in the 1960s. The explanatory introduction is in English as well as Finnish.

474 **Suomen kielen käänteissanakirja. Reverse dictionary of modern standard Finnish.**
Tuomo Tuomi. Helsinki: Finnish Literature Society, 1980. 2nd ed. xxx+546p. (Suomen Kirjallisuuden Seuran toimituksia [Publications of the Finnish Literature Society], 274).

Invaluable for teachers of Finnish, this reverse dictionary prints out all the headwords in *Nykysuomen sanakirja* (q.v.) and has its commentary in English and Finnish.

Courses and grammars

475 **Finnish for foreigners (1, 2 and 3).**
Maija-Hellikki Aaltio. Helsinki: Otava, 1978. 10th ed. 253p.; 1976. 8th rev. ed. 192p.; and 1975. 187p.

This Finnish course (1 and 2) is frequently used in evening classes in Britain. It aims to teach the beginner spoken Finnish and the different constructions used in the written language are considered more briefly. The dialogues which introduce each lesson are practical in character. There are exercises with a key at the end of each book. Word lists and indexes are provided. The reader (book 3) offers a good range of texts in a wide variety of styles together with a glossary. Tapes and cassettes are sold separately to accompany volumes 1 and 2.

476 **Finnish for foreigners 1. Oral drills.**
Maija-Hellikki Aaltio. Helsinki: Otava, 1976. 3rd ed. 78p.

Intended to reinforce the basic declensions and conjugations and the elementary conversation and pronunciation of the first lessons. Tapes or cassettes available separately.

477 **A Finnish grammar.**
John Atkinson. Helsinki: Finnish Literature Society, 1977. 4th ed. 131p.

The student who is accustomed to grammatical terminology will find this book a useful means of acquiring quickly a basic knowledge of the grammar for reading the language without the distractions of large vocabularies. Helpful for reference, too, in spite of the absence of an index.

478 **Finnish.**
Arthur H. Whitney. London: Teach Yourself Books, 1956. reprinted 1979. 301p.

An introduction on pronunciation is followed by twenty lessons, each with grammatical notes, vocabulary, an exercise (Finnish into English, with key at the end of the book), and a reading. The grammar is comprehensive and detailed though the vocabularies are long and tough for the beginner using the book as a self-tutor. The readings are a useful source of texts.

479 **Basic course in Finnish.**
Meri Lehtinen, supervised and edited by Thomas A. Sebeok. Bloomington, Indiana: Indiana University, 1963. xxxiii+657p. (Indiana University Publications. Uralic and Altaic Series, 27).

This massive volume is a revision of Sebeok's *Spoken Finnish* (1947), and is a comprehensive combined grammar and drill book designed to be used in intensive first-year Finnish courses; it is not suitable for self-tuition. There are summaries of grammatical points, declensions and conjugations and a glossary. Cassettes are available.

480 **The Linguaphone Finnish course.**
London: Linguaphone Institute, n.d. 3 books; cassettes or records.

This is a revised version of an old conversational course, with sixty recorded lessons based on familiar or practical situations, which are reproduced in the textbook. There are separate books for vocabulary and grammar. A tutorial service enhances the value of the course.

481 **Suomea suomeksi 1-2.** (Finnish in Finnish 1-2.)
Olli Nuutinen. Helsinki: Suomalaisen Kirjallisuuden Seura, 1978-79. 2 vols. (Vol. 1: 1979. 2nd rev. ed.) (Suomalaisen Kirjallisuuden Seuran toimituksia [Publications of the Finnish Literature Society], 338).

482 **Finnish in Finnish. Vocabulary Suomea suomeksi 1-2.**
Olli Nuutinen, vocabulary in English by Michael O'Dell. Helsinki: Suomalaisen Kirjallisuuden Seura, 1978. 2 vols. (Vol. 1: 2nd ed.).

Suomea suomeksi (previous item) is designed as a one-year taught course in Finnish, producing 'a solid knowledge of Finnish structure and a basic vocabulary of about two thousand words': it uses Finnish only. The vocabularies (*Finnish in Finnish*) are arranged lesson by lesson, Finnish-English, with a single Finnish word-list at the end of each book.

483 **Finnish structural sketch.**
Robert T. Harms. Bloomington, Indiana: Indiana University, 1964. vii+105p. (Indiana University Publications. Uralic and Altaic Series, 42).

'The final or morphophonemic stage of a transformational grammar of spoken standard Finnish.' For the student of linguistics.

484 **Korva tarkkana: kuullun ymmärtämisharjoituksia.** (With a keen ear: listening comprehension exercises.)
Maija-Hellikki Aaltio. Helsinki: Otava, 1977. 102p.

Comprehension exercises, with keys and vocabulary. Tape or cassette available.

485 **Suomen harjoituksia 1.** (Finnish exercises 1.)
Eila Hämäläinen. Helsinki: Suomalaisen Kirjallisuuden Seura, 1978. 149p. (Suomalaisen Kirjallisuuden Seuran toimituksia [Publications of the Finnish Literature Society], 344).

The exercises consist of a drill book and six hours of tapes. They are designed to accompany *Suomea suomeksi 1* (q.v.) but can also be used independently. They take the user from phonetic drills through grammar drills and on to dialogues and comprehension passages. Instructions are given for the student in English, German and Swedish, and for the teacher in Finnish.

486 **Finnish conversational exercises: elementary level.**
Vilho Kallioinen. Helsinki: Suomalaisen Kirjallisuuden Seura, 1974. 164p.

A useful drill book intended for the practice of basic grammar in class.

487 **Suomen kielioppi.** (Finnish grammar.)
Aarni Penttilä. Porvoo, Finland: Werner Söderström, 1963. 2nd rev. ed. 692+36p. bibliog.

The largest and most thorough Finnish grammar.

488 **Suomen kielioppi: äänne- ja sanaoppi. Oppikoulua ja omin päin opiskelua varten.** (Finnish grammar: phonology and morphology. For the grammar school and private study.) E. N. Setälä, Matti Sadeniemi. Helsinki: Otava, 1975. 20th ed. 141p.

An old-established grammar, regularly revised.

489 **Suomen kielen lauseoppi.** (The syntax of the Finnish language.) E. N. Setälä, Matti Sadeniemi. Helsinki: Otava, 1973. 16th ed. 142p.

The basic work on Finnish syntax.

490 **Nykysuomen käsikirja.** (Handbook of modern Finnish.) Edited by Osmo Ikola. Espoo, Finland: Weilin & Göös, 1977. rev. ed. 389p. bibliog.

This is a major source of reference about the basic problems of Finnish grammar and style, with a very useful, partially annotated bibliography, and appendices of foreign words, place-names and common abbreviations.

Readers

491 **Finnish reader and glossary.** Robert Austerlitz. Bloomington, Indiana: Indiana University; The Hague: Mouton, 1966. 2nd ed. xv+294p. (Indiana University Publications. Uralic and Altaic Series, 15).

'Designed for students with some knowledge of Finnish *or* with training in linguistics.' Comprises sixty-nine pages of varied texts plus a crossword puzzle. The extensive glossary, which includes the morphophonemic breakdown of each item occurring in the text, is intended 'to serve as a source of detailed grammatical analysis in addition to its function as a dictionary'.

492 **Finnish literary reader: with notes.** Paavo Ravila. Bloomington, Indiana: Indiana University, 1965. ix+186p. (Indiana University Publications. Uralic and Altaic Series, 44).

'Designed to give the reader a brief picture of the subject matter and style of Finnish writers and poets.' A highly personal choice of prose from Kivi to Huovinen and (separately) of poetry from Leino to Haavikko. Each extract is preceded by a note on the author and his works.

493 **Finnish reader: extracts from modern Finnish literature.**
Edited by Arthur H. Whitney. London: Teach Yourself Books, 1971. 191p.

A convenient, but not representative, series of fifteen texts, extracts from modern Finnish writers (mostly prose), with parallel translations. Intended for those who have worked through the compiler's *Finnish* (q.v.) or some other textbook.

Finnish for foreigners.
See item no. 475.

Swedish

494 **Scandinavian languages.**
M. P. Barnes. In: *A guide to foreign language courses and dictionaries.* Edited by A. J. Walford and J. E. O. Screen. London: Library Association, 1977, 3rd rev. and enl. ed. p. 128-63.

A selective survey of Swedish courses, grammars and dictionaries available at the time of compilation is printed on p. 150-63. The guide is intended for teachers, students and librarians.

495 **Ordbok över Finlands svenska folkmål.** (Dictionary of Swedish dialects in Finland.)
Olav Ahlbäck. Helsinki: Forskningscentralen för de inhemska språken, 1976- . map. bibliog. (Forskningscentralen för de inhemska språken. Skrifter [Research Centre for the Languages of Finland. Publications] 1).

This important dialect dictionary is being compiled from published and unpublished source material dating principally from about 1860 onwards. Of the twenty-one parts planned, two have so far appeared, Vol. I:1 (abbal-bister) in 1976, and Vol. I:2 (bistog-båt) in 1978.

Lapp

496 **Lappische Chrestomathie mit grammatikalischem Abriss und Wörterverzeichnis.** (A Lapp chrestomathy with grammatical summary and glossary.)
Erkki Itkonen. Helsinki: Suomalais-ugrilainen Seura, 1960. X+188p. (Hilfsmittel für das Studium der Finnisch-ugrischen Sprachen, VII).

Contains a chrestomathy, p. 1-40; a grammatical summary, p. 41-72; and a glossary, p. 73-185.

Finno-Ugrian languages and peoples.
See item no. 449.

Survey of the Uralic languages.
See item no. 450.

Literature

General

497 **Suomen kirjallisuus.** (Finnish literature.)
Helsinki: Suomalaisen Kirjallisuuden Seura & Otava, 1963-70. 8 vols. bibliog.

Finnish literature of all types is treated thematically as well as chronologically in this massive and important collective work in Finnish, which is the only full account of its subject. There is an extensive companion anthology, *Suomen kirjallisuuden antologia* (Anthology of Finnish literature) (Helsinki: Otava, 1963-75. 8 vols.).

498 **A history of Finnish literature.**
Jaakko Ahokas. Bloomington, Indiana: Indiana University Research Center for the Language Sciences, for the American-Scandinavian Foundation, 1973. ix+568p.

A personal approach to literature both in Finnish and Swedish, describing writers rather than writing, and arranged by period, with notes on individual authors and their works. Very little on oral tradition. Notes compensate to some extent for the lack of a bibliography.

499 **A nation in search of identity: Finnish literature 1830-1917.**
Irma Rantavaara. In: *Literature and Western civilisation. Volume 5: The modern World. II. Realities.* Edited by David Daiches and Anthony Thorlby. London: Aldus Books, 1972, p. 329-61. bibliog.

'In the process of establishing the national identity, Finnish literature has all along done its best to show the nation its true face - acting as the super-ego, lifting a warning finger when necessary, but also giving moral support in periods of national despair.' A handy survey of the literature of the period and its characteristics.

500 **The two literatures of Finland today.**
World Literature Today: a Literary Quarterly of the University of Oklahoma, vol. 54, no. 1 (winter 1980), p. 5-66. bibliog.

Much of this issue is devoted to an interesting symposium on contemporary Finnish literature, comprising fourteen articles. These include 'Contemporary Finnish literature: general features and main lines' by Kai Laitinen, and bibliographies of articles on, and reviews of, Finnish literature in *World Literature Today* and its precursor *Books Abroad*, from 1935-80 and 1929-79 respectively.

501 **Finlands litteratur efter år 1965.** (Finnish literature after 1965.)
Kai Laitinen, Juhani Niemi, Ingmar Svedberg. Helsinki: Suomen Kirjastoseura, 1975. 71p.

Three essays in Swedish on aspects of the development of Finnish literature during the decade 1965-75. Has a list of contemporary writers with the titles and dates of their works.

502 **[Special issue devoted to modernism in Finland-Swedish literature].**
Scandinavica: an International Journal of Scandinavian Studies. Supplement to vol. 15, no. 1 (May 1976). Edited by Johan Wrede. London, New York: Academic Press, 1976. 124p.

A collection of five essays in English and one in French on different aspects of Finland-Swedish modernism or modernists.

503 **Suomen kirjailijat 1945-1970. Pienoiselämäkerrat. Teosbibliografiat. Tutkimusviitteet.** (Finnish writers 1945-1970. Short biographies. Bibliographies of works. References to studies.)
Edited by Hannu Launonen, Satu Apo, Tuulikki Hannelius, Irma-Riitta Järvinen, Holger Lillqvist. Helsinki: Suomalaisen Kirjallisuuden Seura, 1977. 438p. (Suomalaisen Kirjallisuuden Seuran toimituksia [Publications of the Finnish Literature Society], 332).

A biographical dictionary in Finnish of Finnish writers who started to publish between 1945 and 1970. It is an indispensable starting point for modern Finnish literary studies, particularly because of the inclusion not only of bibliographies of the authors' works but also of references to studies and critical articles about them. Volumes are planned to cover earlier periods.

504 **An island people: a note on Åland writing.**
Thomas Warburton. *Books from Finland*, vol. XI, no. 4 (1977), p. 220-24.

The writers of the Åland Islands can be considered to form a distinctive group in Finland-Swedish literature, very much rooted in their surroundings and realists in their outlook. This article by a writer and publisher describes the work of some of these writers.

505 **The whole place is swarming with blue cats.**
Roderick Dixon. *Look at Finland*, no. 3 (1979), p. 40-45.

An illustrated description of recent writing for children in Finland. The author concludes that literature for children tends to consist of works of imagination that expect children to use their own imagination and intelligence to deal with the ideas and language of the books.

506 **Whodunit: the detective story in Finland.**
Erkka Lehtola. *Books from Finland*, vol. XI, no. 4 (1977), p. 246-51.

Two writers, Mika Waltari and Mauri Sariola, dominate Finnish detective fiction, but others are also described in this short survey of the genre.

507 **The image of the Finn in English and American literature.**
W. R. Mead. *Neuphilologische Mitteilungen*, vol. 64, pt. 3 (1963), p. 243-64.

Mead sorts the characters of Finns in English and American fiction into characteristic types: the characters in occult, heroes in cardboard, prisoners of romance and figures of fun. He notes that the Finn was a negative character to writers of fiction until the present century and shows how Finland has made its greatest impact on the outside world at times of international and domestic stress.

508 **Parnasso.**
Helsinki: Yhtyneet Kuvalehdet, 1951- . eight issues per year.

Literary periodical in Finnish, containing creative prose and poetry in the original and in translation as well as articles on literature, and reviews of books, films and plays.

Books from Finland.
See item no. 723.

Kaunokirjallisuutemme käännöksiä: bibliografinen luettelo suomenkielisen kaunokirjallisuuden käännöksistä. Livres finnois en traduction: romans, nouvelles, poésies, pièces de théâtre. Guide bibliographique. (Finnish literature in translation: a bibliographical list of translations of Finnish-language literature. Finnish books in translation: novels, short stories, poetry, plays. Bibliographical guide.)
See item no. 761.

Oral tradition, *Kalevala*

509 **Finnish folklore research 1828-1918.**
Jouko Hautala. Helsinki: Societas Scientiarum Fennica, 1969. 197p. map. bibliog. (The History of Learning and Science in Finland 1828-1918, 12).

A history of research into Finnish folklore by a leading authority. Extensive list of references.

510 **A hundred years of Finnish folklore research: a reappraisal.**
Lauri Honko. *Folklore*, vol. 90, no. 2 (1979), p. 141-52.

Outlines the recent change in emphasis in Finnish folklore research which has left behind the 'geographical-historical school' - very much the 'Finnish method' of research - to move from epic to ritual poetry, from text to context, from archives to the field, from the human mind to informants and communities, and from comparative to regional studies. There are, moreover, changes in approaches, including such theoretical 'umbrellas' as tradition communication, tradition production, and tradition ecology.

511 **Finnish folkloristics. 1-2.**
Edited by Pentti Leino, Annikki Kaivola-Bregenhöj, Urpo Vento. Helsinki: Suomalaisen Kirjallisuuden Seura, 1974-75. 2 vols. bibliog. (Studia Fennica, 17-18).

These two volumes of the important series *Studia Fennica* provide a survey of contemporary Finnish folkloristics. The article by Outi Lehtipuro 'Trends in Finnish folkloristics' (vol. 2, p. 7-36) considers what subjects have interested and are interesting Finnish folklorists and their approaches to those subjects; it has an extensive bibliography.

512 **Folklore and nationalism in modern Finland.**
William A. Wilson. Bloomington, Indiana; London: Indiana University Press, 1976. xii+272p. maps. bibliog.

An attempt to explain the influence of folklore on Finnish nationalism and its practical consequences for Finnish politics.

513 **Finnish folk poetry.**
Michael Branch. *Books from Finland*, vol. X, nos. 1 and 2 (1976), p. 19-31.

Sets the scene for the anthology of *Finnish folk poetry - epic* (see the following item), of which the author was a compiler. Includes illustrations and the text and translation of one of the items in the anthology. A concise and authoritative introduction to the subject.

514 **Finnish folk poetry - epic: an anthology in Finnish and English.**

Compiled by Matti Kuusi, Keith Bosley, Michael Branch. Helsinki: Suomalaisen Kirjallisuuden Seura, 1977. 607p. map. bibliog. (Publications of the Finnish Literature Society, 329).

Finnish oral tradition, particularly folk poetry, has immense significance in Finnish literature. This collection of epic folk poetry, which is thematically arranged, gives a selection of poems in Finnish and English. The extensive introduction and other critical apparatus are in English.

515 **Finnish folklore reader and glossary.**

Elli Köngäs Maranda. Bloomington, Indiana: Indiana University; The Hague: Mouton, 1968. [xxv]+337p. (Indiana University Publications. Uralic and Altaic Series, 71).

A useful classified selection of folklore texts (p. 1-83) made on the basis of their suitability for use in language learning. Every word in the texts is entered in the glossary (p. 85-328) in its occurrent form.

516 **Tales from a Finnish fireside.**

James Cloyd Bowman, Margery Bianco, from a translation by Aili Kolehmainen. London: Chatto & Windus, 1975. 159p.

A collection of twenty-six Finnish folk tales, divided into tales of magic, droll stories, and fables. Originally published as *Tales from a Finnish tupa* (Chicago: Albert Whiteman, 1936) and subsequently reprinted.

517 **Arvoitukset. Finnish riddles.**

Edited by Leea Virtanen, Annikki Kaivola-Bregenhøj, Aarre Nyman. Helsinki: Suomalaisen Kirjallisuuden Seura, 1977. 287p. map. bibliog.

An anthology of 1,248 true riddles known to Finnish tradition, taken from the Folklore Archives of the Finnish Literature Society. Editorial principles and introductory chapters are in English as well as Finnish. Translations of the riddles; index of answers (in English).

518 **Children's lore.**

Leea Virtanen. Helsinki: Suomalaisen Kirjallisuuden Seura, 1978. 100p. bibliog. (Studia Fennica, 22).

This study of school children's traditions - their activities, rhymes, games, teasing and beliefs - is based on the study of Finnish children but has a broader approach to the significance of children's lore in general.

519 **Väinämöinen, eternal sage.**
Martti Haavio. Porvoo, Finland: Werner Söderström, 1952. 277p. map. bibliog.

A scholarly study of the Väinämöinen (chief legendary hero) not of *Kalevala* (see the following item) but of folk poetry in general. The book stresses in particular the image of Väinämöinen presented in surviving folk poetry fragments.

520 **Epic of the North: the story of Finland's *Kalevala*.**
John I. Kolehmainen. New York Mills, Minnesota: Northwestern Publishing Co., 1973. iii+386p. bibliog.

This is a general account of the history of *Kalevala*, the national epic of Finland, the first edition of which appeared in 1835. The book also deals with the singers of *Kalevala*, and the influence of the epic on Finnish culture, which has been tremendous. It is especially good on the personalities of the singers of folklore, and has a discursive bibliography.

521 **The Balto-Finnic epics.**
Felix J. Oinas. In: *Heroic epic and saga: an introduction to the world's great folk epics*. Edited by Felix J. Oinas. Bloomington, Indiana; London: Indiana University Press, 1978, p. 286-309. bibliog.

Describes the compilation of *Kalevala*, its synopsis, composition and form. Also describes the Estonian *Kalevipoeg*. Annotated bibliography.

522 **The *Kalevala* and its background.**
Björn Collinder. *Arv: tidskrift för Nördisk folkminnesforskning. Journal of Scandinavian Folklore*, vol. 20 (1964), p. 1-112. bibliog.

Written for an American audience, this provides a scholarly but easily assimilated account of the background of *Kalevala*. It has also been published separately (Stockholm: Almqvist & Wiksell, 1964. 112p.).

523 ***Kalevala*: the land of the heroes.**
Translated from the Finnish by W. F. Kirby, introduction by J. B. C. Grundy. London: Dent, 1977. 2 vols. in 1 (vii+327; [ii]+285p.). (Everyman's Library, 259).

This easily obtainable translation of the epic was originally published in 1907.

524 **The *Kalevala*, or poems of the Kalevala district.**
Compiled by Elias Lönnrot, prose translation with foreword and appendices by Francis Peabody Magoun, Jr. Cambridge, Massachusetts: Harvard University Press, 1963. reprinted, 1970. xxiv+413p. map. bibliog.

In addition to the translation itself, this volume includes appendices on Elias Lönnrot (1802-84), the original collector and creator of *Kalevala*, and translations of his prefaces, as well as appendices on the origin and influence of *Kalevala*, with the mention of various bibliographical references.

525 **The *Old Kalevala* and certain antecedents.**
Compiled by Elias Lönnrot, prose translations with foreword and appendices by Francis Peabody Magoun, Jr. Cambridge, Massachusetts: Harvard University Press, 1969. xx+312p. map.

This is a translation of *Kalevala* as printed by Lönnrot in 1835 (as distinct from the 'New' 1849 version). It includes a glossary of proper names, and concordances linking the Old and New *Kalevala*, and the Proto-*Kalevala* of 1834 with the Old *Kalevala*. Important as a means of finding out about the Old *Kalevala*.

526 **The song of Aino: *Kalevala* iv.**
Translated from the Finnish by Keith Bosley. High Wycombe, England: Moonbird, 1973. 28p.

An interesting modern translation of one of the most poignant episodes of *Kalevala*.

527 **Tales from the long lakes: Finnish legends from the *Kalevala*.**
Keith Bosley. London: Gollancz, 1966. 144p. map.

A retelling for young readers of many of the *Kalevala* stories. In prose.

528 **Heroes of the *Kalevala*: Finland's saga.**
Babette Deutsch. New York: Julian Messner, 1971. 13th printing. 238p. bibliog.

Kalevala retold for children: 'the effort throughout has been to preserve as nearly as possible in a straightforward prose narrative the character of the original'.

529 **Heroes of *Kalevala*.**
Irma Kaplan. London: Frederick Muller, 1973. 63p.

A retelling of seven of the *Kalevala* stories for children.

530 ***Kalevala*: heroic tales from Finland.**
Ursula Synge. London: Bodley Head, 1977. 222p.

A prose version of parts of *Kalevala*, retold for children.

Ancient cultures of the Uralian peoples.
See item no. 102.

Anthologies

531 **Voices from Finland: an anthology of Finland's verse and prose in English, Finnish and Swedish.**
Edited by Elli Tompuri. Helsinki: Sanoma, 1947. 296p.

Compiled with the aims of introducing English-speaking readers to the literature of Finland and of recalling it to Finns abroad. Poetry is reproduced in the original as well as in translation; prose in translation only. There are sections on *Kalevala* and *Kanteletar* (an anthology of folk poetry also produced by Lönnrot). Finnish writers in Finnish and Swedish are represented, including a selection of what were then recent works in addition to older poems and a selection of modern poetry and prose. There is a historical introduction. The anthology is still worth reading.

532 **Finnish Odyssey: poetry and folk songs of Finland in translation. With poems of tribute and drawings.**
Robert Armstrong. London: Research Publishing Co., 1975. 104p.

Includes translations of seventeen Finnish poets (almost all writing in Finnish) from Runeberg and Kianto to Haavikko and Saarikoski, some folk songs and Christmas songs, and some portions of *Kalevala*.

533 **Snow in May: an anthology of Finnish writing 1945-1972.**
Richard Dauenhauer, Philip Binham. Rutherford, New Jersey: Fairleigh Dickinson University Press; London: Associated University Presses, 1978. 389p. bibliog.

The first major anthology of modern Finnish literature in English. Nine introductory essays - including an important contribution by Professor Kai Laitinen - precede sections on poetry, prose and drama. Post-war Finnish and Swedish writers are represented and there is an appendix of short biographies of those included as well as a short bibliography. The selection of material has been criticized as unbalanced, and some of the translations have been faulted, but this remains a notable and accessible collection.

534 **Swedo-Finnish stories.**
Translated from the Swedish with an introduction by George C. Schoolfield. New York: Twayne and the American-Scandinavian Foundation, 1974. [viii]+338p. (Library of Scandinavian Literature, 27).

A varied selection of stories from writers ranging (chronologically) from Sara Wacklin to Johan Bargum. There is a general introduction on Swedish-language literature in Finland and on the short story as well as notes on each author represented.

535 **Baltic literature: a survey of Finnish, Estonian, Latvian and Lithuanian literatures.**
Aleksis Rubulis. Notre Dame, Indiana; London: University of Notre Dame Press, 1970. xv+215p.

Finnish literature, p. 1-53. A mixture of brief historical notes and extracts, some quite long, from *Kalevala* and a variety of authors writing in Finnish and Swedish, although there is very little on post-war writing.

536 **Modern Nordic plays: Finland.**
New York: Twayne, 1973. 304p. (Library of Scandinavian Literature, 17).

Four modern plays, with an introduction by Professor Kai Laitinen. The plays are: *The superintendent* by Paavo Haavikko, translated by Philip Binham; *Eva Maria* by V. V. Järner, translated by Dympna Connolly (the only one of the collection originally in Swedish); *Snow in May* by Eeva-Liisa Manner, translated by Philip Binham; and *Private Jokinen's marriage leave* by Veijo Meri, translated by J. R. Pitkin.

Individual writers

537 **In the dark, move slowly.**
Tuomas Anhava, poems selected and translated from the Finnish by Anslem Hollo. London: Cape Goliard, 1969. [40]p.

The anthology of poems by Anhava (born 1927) from which this selection is taken was published in 1967.

538 **The wide wings of summer.**
Bo Carpelan, translated from the Swedish by Sheila La Farge. London: Heinemann, 1972. [iv]+121p.

539 **Bow Island.**
Bo Carpelan, translated from the Swedish by Sheila La Farge. New York: Dell, 1974. 159p. (Laurel-Leaf Library).

This volume and the preceding item are the same book with different titles. Published as *Bagen* in 1968, this is a story for children about children on the Finnish coast. Carpelan (born 1926) is one of the leading contemporary writers in Swedish in Finland.

540 **Glimpses into the past and the present.**
Tito Colliander, interview by W. Glyn Jones. *Books from Finland*, vol. XIII, no. 1 (1979), p. 22-28.

An interview which reveals something of the literary and religious views of Tito Colliander, a notable Swedish-Finnish novelist, short story and memoir writer (born 1904).

541 **Selected poems: Paavo Haavikko translated and with an introduction by Anselm Hollo; Tomas Tranströmer translated and with an introduction by Robin Fulton.**
Paavo Haavikko, Tomas Tranströmer. Harmondsworth, England: Penguin Books, 1974. 141p. (Penguin Modern European Poets).

Haavikko, p. 9-66. Paavo Haavikko (born 1931) is characterized in Anselm Hollo's introduction as 'the most original of the poets who first published their work in the 1950's'.

542 ***The horseman*: the libretto of the opera composed by Aulis Sallinen.**
Paavo Haavikko, translated from the Finnish by Philip Binham. Lahti, Finland: Esan Kirjapaino, 1974. 119p.

A parallel text and translation of *Ratsumies*, an opera set partly in Novgorod, partly at Olavinlinna (where it was first performed for the fifth centenary celebrations of the castle), and partly elsewhere in Finland: 'a tale that tells of a man and a woman, of war, horses, women, luck, death'.

543 **My books and characters.**
Tove Jansson, interview by W. Glyn Jones. *Books from Finland*, vol. XII, no. 3 (1978), p. 90-97.

Professor W. Glyn Jones of the University of Newcastle upon Tyne is engaged on a biography of Jansson, author and artist whose work for adults has received acclaim along with her more famous Moomin books for children.

544 **Finn family Moomintroll.**
Tove Jansson. Harmondsworth, England: Penguin Books, 1961. reprinted, 1979. 156p.

Included here as an example of the highly popular and much-translated Moomin books which have delighted children in many countries.

545 **Maria Jotuni: money, morals and love.**
Irmeli Niemi. *Books from Finland*, vol. XIV, no. 1 (1980), p. 20-26.

Maria Jotuni (1880-1943) achieved her greatest artistic successes as a dramatist and her plays have been very popular in Finland.

546 **Aino Kallas (1878-1956): ambassador extraordinary.**
Kai Laitinen. *Books from Finland*, vol. XII, no. 4 (1978), p. 159-63.

Aino Kallas was a figure in literary life during the 1920s in London, where her husband was Estonian minister. She was much acclaimed as a writer, and this is a short but authoritative account of her life and writings.

547 **Three novels.**

Aino Kallas, translated from the Finnish by Alex Matson. Helsinki: Otava, 1974. 219p.

Comprises three of the best-known of Aino Kallas's novels: *Barbara von Tisenhausen*; *The Rector of Reigi*; and *The wolf's bride.*

548 **Extending the bounds of reality: an approach to the work of Christer Kihlman.**

Ingmar Svedberg. *Books from Finland*, vol. X, nos. 1 and 2 (1976), p. 7-10.

An assessment of the work of an influential contemporary Swedish-Finnish writer.

549 **Tamara.**

Eeva Kilpi, translated from the Finnish by Philip Binham. New York: Delacorte Press/Seymour Lawrence, 1978. 233p. (A Merloyd Lawrence Book).

A story of a woman's love and loves, originally published in 1972 by a leading contemporary woman writer (born 1928).

550 **Seven brothers: a novel.**

Aleksis Kivi, translated from the Finnish by Alex Matson, translation of 3rd edition revised by Irma Rantavaara. Helsinki: Tammi, 1973. 3rd ed. 342p.

Irma Rantavaara also contributed a short foreword about the book which for the non-Finnish reader is characterized as 'a key to the Finnish national character', by 'Finland's best-known author', Aleksis Kivi (1834-72).

551 **Eino Leino, 1878-1926.**

Annamari Sarajas. *Books from Finland*, vol. XII, no. 2 (1978), p. 40-46.

A Finnish literary scholar's assessment of both volumes of Leino's *Whitsongs* (see the following item), including translations into English by Keith Bosley and into French by Gabriel Rebourcet.

552 **Whitsongs.**

Eino Leino, translated from the Finnish by Keith Bosley, introduction by Michael Branch. London: Menard Press, 1978. 79p.

An important introduction precedes a powerful translation of what is generally held to be Leino's poetic masterpiece which he published in 1903.

553 **Väinö Linna: a classic in his own time.**
Yrjö Varpio. *Books from Finland*, vol. XI, no. 3 (1977), p. 192-97. bibliog.

Väinö Linna has, more than any other modern Finnish novelist, influenced the country's approach to its immediate past. His novel *The unknown soldier* (translated into English, q.v.) gives a vivid impression of the Continuation War (1941-44); *Here under the North Star* (regrettably not available in English, but see *Ici, sous l'étoile polaire*) describes the influence of events on a village up to and including the Civil War of 1918. This short account of Linna's work and place in Finnish literature includes a bibliography of translations.

554 **Väinö Linna and the Finnish condition.**
Marvin Rintala. *Journal of Baltic Studies*, vol. 8, no. 3 (fall 1977), p. 223-31.

An American political scientist's view of Linna's war novels, suggesting that in *Here under the North Star* Linna produced the great Finnish epic novel, explaining the social and political history of modern Finland.

555 **The unknown soldier.**
Väinö Linna. Porvoo, Finland: Werner Söderström, 1975. reprinted. xiv+310p.

An immensely successful novel (first published in 1954) about a group of soldiers in the Continuation War of 1941-44. This translation published in Finland is a slight improvement on that published in London by Collins and in New York by Putnam in 1957.

556 **Ici, sous l'étoile polaire. (Täällä Pohjantähden alla).** (Here under the North Star.)
Väinö Linna, French translation from the Finnish by Jean-Jacques Fol. Paris: Robert Laffont, 1962-63. vols. 1 and 2. map. (Collection 'Pavillons').

Of Linna's greatest works only *The unknown soldier* is widely known in the West outside Scandinavia. The first two volumes of the trilogy *Here under the North Star* have been translated into French (volume II with a historical introduction by the translator), but not into English. An extract from this novel, which describes the impact of events on a Finnish village up to and including the Civil War of 1918, has been translated in *Snow in May* (q.v.), p. 232-48.

557 **The song of the blood-red flower.**
Johannes Linnankoski. London: Gyldendal, 1920. [vi]+285p.

The original, published in 1905, is a major prose work of the neo-romantic period, combining Shavian radicalism with Beardsley-like surrealism.

558 **My childhood.**
Toivo Pekkanen, translated from the Finnish by Alan Blair, with an introduction by Thomas Warburton. Madison and Milwaukee, Wisconsin; London: University of Wisconsin Press, 1966. xvii+250p. (Nordic Translation Series).

Lapsuuteni (My childhood) is one of the last works (published in 1953) of one 'of the first writers to represent a "new" generation of the Finnish working class'. The novel is characterized by Warburton as 'the book of a wise, understanding, and clear-sighted man'.

559 **The long distance patrol.**
Paavo Rintala, translated from the Finnish by Maurice Michael. London: Allen & Unwin, 1967. 184p.

A translation of *Sissiluutnantti* (1963), a front-line story set in the last war.

560 **J. L. Runeberg.**
Tore Wretö, translated in collaboration with the author by Zalek S. Herman. Boston, Massachusetts: Twayne, 1980. 186p. bibliog. (Twayne's World Authors Series, 503).

This new introduction to Johan Ludvig Runeberg (1804-77) and his writing presents him in his different literary roles, 'as critic, short story writer, epic poet, lyrist, poet of the nation, and dramatist'. The author considers that 'as a creator of ideals and as a source of style, Runeberg is one of the most significant Scandinavian authors'.

561 **The tales of Ensign Stål.**
Johan Ludvig Runeberg, illustrated by Albert Edelfelt, with an introduction by Yrjö Hirn. Helsinki: Söderström, 1952. xxvi+244p.

This is one of the most influential collections of poetry to be published in Finland. Runeberg, who wrote in Swedish, inspired generations of Finns with his patriotic poems. The translations here are by Charles Wharton Stork, Clement Burbank Shaw and C. D. Broad. Edelfelt's illustrations are famous.

562 **Helsinki: selected poems.**
Pentti Saarikoski, translated from the Finnish by Anselm Hollo. London: Rapp & Carroll, 1967. 48p.

Poems by 'the most-talked-about and best-known poet of his generation in Finland', to quote Anselm Hollo's introduction. Saarikoski was born in 1937.

563 **The tale of Katrina.**
Sally Salminen, translated by Naomi Walford. London: Readers' Union, with Thornton Butterworth, 1938. 384p.

The best work by Salminen (1906-76). A novel in Swedish about the hard life of a sailor's wife.

564 **The Helsinki affair.**
Mauri Sariola, translated from the Finnish by Alan Blair. London: Cassell, 1970. [iv]+170p.

Translation of *Lavean tien laki* (originally published in 1961). The author is perhaps the best-known writer of detective stories in Finland.

565 **Fallen asleep while young: the history of the last offshoot of an old family tree.**
F. E. Sillanpää, translated from the Finnish by Alexander Matson. London: Putnam, 1933. 314p.

A translation of *Nuorena nukkunut*, originally published in Finnish in 1931. The story of a girl who dies young of consumption. The translation was also published as *The maid Silja* (New York: Macmillan, 1933. 314p.). This is the best-known of the novels by Sillanpää, who won the Nobel prize for literature in 1939.

566 **Meek heritage: a novel.**
F. E. Sillanpää, originally translated by Alexander Matson, revised by John R. Pitkin. Helsinki: Otava, 1971. 221p.

A translation of *Hurskas kurjuus*, originally published in 1919, and which uses flash-back technique to tell the story of a crofter whose eventual involvement on the Red side in the Civil War cost him his life. The translation by Matson was first published in London (Putnam, 1938. [vii]+280p.) and New York (Knopf, 1938. [vii]+274p.).

567 **People in the summer night: an epic suite. Ihmiset suviyössä.**
F. E. Sillanpää, translated from the Finnish by Alan Blair, with an introduction by Thomas Warburton. Madison and Milwaukee, Wisconsin; London: University of Wisconsin Press, 1966. xviii+158p. (Nordic Translation Series).

'Sillanpää's last work of undiminished strength', published in 1934, is a collection of episodes about people held together by a fight and manslaughter. Helpful introduction and bibliography.

568 **Edith Södergran: a pioneer of Finland-Swedish modernism.**
Gladys Hird. *Books from Finland*, vol. XII, no. 1 (1978), p. 4-7.

Södergran (1892-1923) published only four small volumes of verse and a collection of aphorisms, but introduced modernism to Scandinavia and Finland. Her style appeals more to modern readers than it did to her contemporary critics.

569 **Snobs' Island.**
Henrik Tikkanen, translated from the Swedish by Mary Sandbach. London: Chatto & Windus, 1980. xvii+122p.

A translation of Tikkanen's autobiographical novel *Brandövägen 8 Brandö Tel. 35* (1976), set in the 1920s and 1930s, which established his reputation as a writer.

An introduction by the translator sets the scene to some extent. Tikkanen was born in 1924.

570 **The Sea King's gift and other tales from Finland.**
Zacharius Topelius, retold by Irma Kaplan. London: Frederick Muller, 1973. 137p.

Taken from a collection of poems, stories and fairy tales, *Läsning för barn* (Readings for children), originally published by Topelius (1818-98) in 1865-96. This selection of eight stories conveys the author's power as a storyteller, though he was much more than just a writer for children.

571 **Poems from *Gičča ijat čuov 'gadat* (The last nights of spring) and *Lávlo vizar biello-cizaš* (Sing, chirrup, little bird).**
Nils-Aslak Valkeapää, translated from the Lapp by Keith Bosley, Hannele Branch. *Books from Finland*, vol. XI, no. 2 (1977), p. 134-39.

Included as an example of the work of a modern Lapp poet (born 1943).

572 **Mika Waltari has always been with us.**
Juha Tanttu. *Look at Finland*, no. 1 (1979), p. 50-51.

Alas, Mika Waltari, perhaps the best-known Finnish writer abroad, is no longer with us since he died in 1979. This is a brief note of his life and publications.

573 **Mika Waltari ulkomailla: käännösten bibliografia. Mika Waltari utomlands: bibliografi av översättningar. Mika Waltari abroad: bibliography of translations.**
J. Vallinkoski, A. Juurinen, introduction by Panu Rajala. Helsinki: Helsingin yliopiston kirjasto, 1978. [iv] + 79p. (Helsingin yliopiston kirjaston julkaisuja. Helsingfors universitetsbiblioteks skrifter. Publications of the University Library at Helsinki, 40).

A bibliography of translations with an introduction by Panu Rajala in Finnish, Swedish and English. The bibliography is divided into separate works, short stories and essays, plays, poems. There is a title index of translations and an index of persons.

574 **Sinuhe, the Egyptian: a novel.**
Mika Waltari, translated by Naomi Walford. London: Putnam, 1949. [vi]+503p.

A translation of *Sinuhe, egyptiläinen* (published in 1945), the most successful universal best-seller in Finnish literature. It is a historical novel set in ancient Egypt. There are numerous editions, and the book has also been published in translation as *The Egyptian*.

575 **A stranger came to the farm.**
Mika Waltari, translated by Naomi Walford. London: Putnam, 1953. 243p.

Set in Finland, this novel (*Vieras mies tuli taloon*, published in 1937), with its tragic theme, caused a considerable stir when it first appeared. Other editions have been issued.

576 **The dark angel.**
Mika Waltari, translated by Naomi Walford. London: Putnam, 1953. 320p.

Perhaps Waltari's greatest success after *Sinuhe*. Originally published as *Johannes Angelos* (1952), this is a historical novel dealing with the siege of Constantinople in 1453. Various editions have been issued.

577 **The Etruscan: a novel.**
Mika Waltari, translated by Evelyn Ramsden. London: Putnam, 1957. 480p.

Translation of *Turms, kuolematon* (1955), a historical novel about the Etruscans, with a strong mystical undercurrent. Other editions have been issued.

578 **The Roman: the memoirs of Minutus Lausus Manilianus.**
Mika Waltari. London: Hodder & Stoughton, 1966. 638p.

This historical novel, originally *Ihmiskunnan viholliset* (1964), deals with the early years of Christianity. Other editions have been issued.

The Arts

Cultural policy and the arts

579 **Cultural policy in Finland: a study prepared under the auspices of the Finnish National Commission for Unesco.**
Paris: UNESCO, 1972. 73p. (Studies and Documents on Cultural Policies).

A brief but broad survey of Finnish cultural policy, embracing descriptions of the administration of the arts, of state support for individual writers and artists, architecture, crafts and design, theatre, literature, music, the visual arts, film and photographic art, libraries, the press and broadcasting.

580 **Art in Finland. Les beaux-arts finlandais. Die bildende Kunst in Finnland.**
Sakari Saarikivi, Kerttu Niilonen, Hilding Ekelund. Helsinki: Otava, 1967. 6th ed. 157p.

On painting and sculpture, industrial art (design), and architecture, with black-and-white illustrations, and text and captions in English, French and German.

581 **Finnish art.**
Onni Okkonen. Porvoo, Finland: Werner Söderström, 1946. 42+[2]+208p.

A representative collection of black-and-white illustrations of architecture, painting and sculpture, preceded by a longish introduction by a notable Finnish art historian.

582 **Kuvia katoavasta Suomesta. Det Finland som försvinner. Pictures of vanishing Finland.**
Edited by Marta Hirn. Helsinki: Weilin & Göös, 1970. 148p.

A selection of the drawings and paintings made in the course of eight expeditions sent out by the Finnish Archaeological Society between 1871 and 1902 to record Finnish architecture and pictorial arts. Buildings, exteriors and interiors, objects of all kinds, in greater and lesser detail, present an evocation of Finland that was already old at the turn of the last century. Introduction and picture captions in English; notes in Finnish and Swedish only.

583 **Finland creates: the inter-relationship of land and design in Finland.**
Jack Fields, David Moore. Jyväskylä, Finland: Gummerus, 1977. 132p.

Attractive and often unusual photographs draw parallels between natural and man-made objects. The book looks at the landscape of Finland and at the work of a number of architects, designers and artists.

Visual arts

584 **Art in Finland: survey of a century.**
Edited by Alf Krohn. Helsinki: Tuli, 1953. 126p.

Several essays by leading Finnish art historians on Finnish painting, sculpture and graphic art during the last hundred years. According to Boulton Smith (see the following item), this remains the most comprehensive account of its subject in English.

585 **The golden age of Finnish art: art nouveau and the national spirit.**
John Boulton Smith. Helsinki: Ministry for Foreign Affairs, 1976. 180p. bibliog.

A very well illustrated account, by a British authority on the period, of the various branches of art in Finland at the end of the 19th and the beginning of the 20th century when Finnish art burgeoned. The bibliography (p. 176) of works in English or with summaries in English is partially annotated and most valuable.

586 **Modern Finnish painting and graphic art.**
John Boulton Smith. London: Weidenfeld & Nicolson, 1970. 48+62p.

Covers the period from the 1890s to the 1960s, concisely and with well-chosen illustrations.

587 **Suomen piirustustaide Lauréuksesta Ekelundiin. Finnish drawings from Lauréus to Ekelund.**
Porvoo, Finland: Werner Söderström, 1966. xxxv+207p.

Compiled under the auspices of the Society of Finnish Graphic Artists Grafia, this is a useful pictorial account of the work of artists born in the 18th and 19th centuries. Includes a shortened English version of the Finnish introduction.

588 **Graphic art in Finland.**
Jouko Tolvanen. Helsinki: Society of Finnish Graphic Artists, 1956. xv+46p.

Although short, this is considered by the British authority Boulton Smith to be the best general account.

589 **Kuvataiteilijat: Suomen kuvataiteilijoiden henkilöhakemisto 1972.** (Pictorial artists: biographical dictionary of Finnish pictorial artists 1972.)
Helsinki: Suomen taiteilijaseura (the Artists' Association of Finland); Porvoo, Finland: Werner Söderström, 1972. [vii]+317p.

This is a comprehensive dictionary of past and present Finnish painters, sculptors and graphic artists, giving brief biographical notes, and information about works and exhibitions. The Finnish-English guide to the abbreviations, though not always accurate, will facilitate use of the Finnish text by the determined English reader.

590 **Finno-Ugric folk art.**
István Rácz, introduction by Niilo Valonen. Helsinki: Otava, 1979. 336p. maps. bibliog.

Places the Finns and the Lapps in their Finno-Ugrian context as far as their folk art is concerned. The introduction by Professor Niilo Valonen (p. 7-28) precedes numerous photographs (in black-and-white and colour) selected by István Rácz, mostly depicting objects in the collections of the National Museum of Finland. There are notes on the photographs (p. 313-36). Originally published as *Suomalais-ugrilaista kansantaidetta* (Helsinki: Otava, 1977).

591 **Treasures of Finnish folk art.**
István Rácz, introduction and notes on the illustrations by Niilo Valonen. Helsinki: Otava, 1969. 230p.

Originally published in Finnish as *Suomen kansantaiteen aarteita* (Helsinki: Otava, 1963). Comprises the introduction (p. 5-15), illustrations (nos. 1-210), and notes on the plates (p. 217-30). Buildings, costumes, textiles and interior decoration are all covered. An excellent all-round impression of the subject.

592 **Early Finnish art from prehistory to the Middle Ages.**
István Rácz, introduction by C. F. Meinander, notes on the illustrations by Pirkko-Liisa Lehtosalo. Helsinki: Otava, 1967. 176p.

Originally published in Finnish as *Kivikirves ja hopearisti: Suomen esihistorian taideaarteita* (Stone axe and silver cross: art treasures of Finnish prehistory) (Helsinki: Otava, 1961). Contains 'A review of Finnish prehistory', by C. F. Meinander (p. 7-19), plates, some coloured (p. 21-164), and notes on the plates (with museum references and dimensions of the objects), (p. 165-76). Fine photographs and a useful introduction and notes.

593 **Art treasures of medieval Finland.**
István Rácz, introduction and notes on the pictures by Riitta Pylkkänen. Helsinki: Otava, 1961. 244p.

Excellent photographs, mostly black-and-white, with a short introduction and useful notes.

594 **Art treasures of the Eastern Orthodox Church of Finland in the Kuopio Orthodox Church Museum.**
István Rácz. Helsinki: Otava, 1971. 131p.

Reveals something of Finland's Orthodox religious tradition and its art. Introduction and captions in Finnish and English.

595 **Treasures of Finnish renaissance and baroque art.**
István Rácz, introduction and notes on the illustrations by Nils Cleve. Helsinki: Otava, 1969. 229p.

Originally published as *Suomen renessanssin ja barokin taideaarteita* (Helsinki: Otava, 1967). Covers the period 1550-1721. The short introduction (p. 5-15) surveys the period in general. There are 209 illustrations of a high quality and useful notes on the plates (p. 217-29).

596 **Modern Finnish sculpture.**
Göran Schildt. London: Weidenfeld & Nicolson, 1970. 55+64p.

A short but well-illustrated account of Finnish sculpture in the 20th century.

597 **Sculptures of Alvar Aalto.**
Göran Schildt. Helsinki: Otava, 1967. 46p.

Describes and depicts some of the famous architect's nonarchitectural work: moulded wood sculptures, furniture legs, monumental sculptures and gold jewellery.

598 **The *ryijy*-rugs of Finland: a historical study.**
U. T. Sirelius. Helsinki: Otava, 1926. [xii]+251p. 93 plates. map.

The standard history and description of the *ryijy* rug in Finland, written by one of Finland's leading ethnographers. Has notes but no bibliography. The *ryijy*, a pile-woven woollen textile, was originally used as a bed cover but is now used as a decorative wall hanging.

599 **The use and traditions of mediaeval rugs and coverlets in Finland.**
Riitta Pylkkänen. Helsinki: Archaeological Society of Finland, 1974. 154p. map. bibliog.

Contains two scholarly studies: 'From counterpane to funeral pall', and 'Ryijy-rug traditions from the 16th and 17th centuries', which together form a richly illustrated account of these textiles, their designs, and use.

600 **Suomalaisia tekstiilejä. Finska textiler. Finnish textiles. Finnische Textilien.**
Anna-Liisa Ahmavaara. Helsinki: Otava, 1970. 88p.

Comprises sections on coverlets (*raanut*), *rya* (*ryijy*) rugs, *täkänä* double weaves, picture weaves, rugs, printed fabrics, furnishing fabrics, everyday textiles, mats, transparent weaves, and dresses. Introduction and descriptions of the illustrations (colour and black-and-white) in Finnish, Swedish, English and German.

601 **Finnish textiles.**
Martha Saarto. Leigh-on-Sea, England: F. Lewis, 1954. 20p. 96 plates.

Good black-and-white illustrations of textiles of various kinds, from *ryijy* rugs to furnishing fabrics and ecclesiastical vestments, with notes on each. There is a short general introduction.

602 **Handweaving patterns from Finland: 122 useful projects for the home and the studio.**
Helvi Pyysalo, Viivi Merisalo. Newton, Massachusetts: Charles T. Branford, 1960. [51]p.

A practical illustrated guide to weaving fabrics of various kinds.

603 **Finnish jewellery and silverware: an introduction to contemporary work and design.**
John Haycraft. Helsinki: Otava, 1962. 64p.

A short description of modern Finnish jewellery, Kalevala jewellery (based on traditional designs), church silver, and the work of the notable designers Bertil Gardberg and Tapio Wirkkala.

604 **Finnish glass.**
Kerttu Niilonen. Helsinki: Tammi, 1967. 112p.

A brief history of glass-making in Finland followed by a more detailed account of notable modern Finnish artists in glass-making. Numerous illustrations.

605 **A century of Finnish ceramics.**
Desmond Smith. *Look at Finland*, no. 4 (1973), p. 6-13.
A popular article to mark the centenary of the famous Arabia ceramics works.

606 **Handicraft renaissance.**
Sinikka Salokorpi. *Look at Finland*, no. 2 (1979), p. 2-11.
A commemorative article for the centenary of the Friends of Finnish Handicraft, with good illustrations, particularly of recent handicraft products.

607 **Modern Scandinavian furniture.**
Ulf Hård af Segerstad. Copenhagen: Gyldendalske Boghandel, 1963. 131p.
Not, of course, confined to Finnish furniture, but looks at the Scandinavian scene as a whole and shows how Finland fits into the pattern of modern style. Very good pictures.

608 **Finnish furniture.**
Sinikka Salokorpi. *Look at Finland*, no. 6 (1973), p. 32-45.
A well-illustrated description of different types of modern Finnish furniture.

609 **Vaivaisukot. Finnish pauper sculptures.**
Markus Leppo. Porvoo, Finland: Werner Söderström, 1967. 148p.
Depicts the pauper collection boxes to be seen at the entrances to many churches in midwestern Finland. A shortened version of the introduction appears in English.

610 **Finland's wooden men-at-alms. Finlands fattiggubbar. Suomen vaivaisukot.**
Markus Leppo. Helsinki: Valokuvakirja-Photobook, 1979. 64p.
A collection of black-and-white photographs of some of the 119 surviving wooden collecting boxes in the form of a statue which have been traced in Finland by the author. Brief introduction in English, Swedish and Finnish.

Design

611 **Finnish design 1875-1975: 100 years of Finnish industrial design.**
Timo Sarpaneva, Erik Bruun, Erik Kruskopf. Helsinki: Otava, 1975. 130p.

A commemorative volume of the centenary of the Finnish Society of Crafts and Design. Describes and illustrates the development of Finnish design from its modest beginnings to the triumphs of the 1950s and its present standing.

612 **A hundred years of Finnish design.**
Erik Kruskopf. *Look at Finland*, no. 1 (1976), p. 12-29.

A richly illustrated article to mark the centenary of the Finnish Society of Crafts and Design. Describes the history of the society and the recent achievements of Finnish design.

613 **Modern Finnish design.**
Ulf Hård af Segerstad. London: Weidenfeld & Nicolson, 1969. [48]+63p.

A concise, general account of Finnish design in the 20th century.

614 **Finnish design: facts and fancy.**
Donald J. Willcox. New York: Van Nostrand Reinhold, 1973. 48+[109]p.

The photographs show a wide range of objects; breathless introduction.

615 **The Ornamo book of Finnish design.**
Helsinki: Ornamo & Finnish Society of Crafts and Design, 1962. 135p.

Published to celebrate the fiftieth anniversary of Ornamo, a society formed to develop domestic crafts and design, this book - consisting mainly of illustrations - shows many facets of Finnish design of the 1950s and early 1960s: fabrics, posters, buttons - nothing seems forgotten.

616 **Suomalaista käyttögrafiikka. Finnish graphic design.**
Porvoo, Finland: Werner Söderström, 1963. 111p.

Covers a considerable range - book illustrations and jackets, pictures in marketing and advertising, coats of arms, bookplates, postage stamps, even restaurant menus. The illustrations are the core of the book which was issued to celebrate the thirtieth anniversary of Grafia, the Society of Finnish Graphic Artists. There are English summaries of the introductory chapters.

617 **Designed in Finland.**
Helsinki: Finnish Foreign Trade Association, 1961- . annual.

A glossy review of Finnish design aimed at the promotion of exports.

618 **Scandinavian design: objects of a life style.**
Eileene Harrison Beer. New York: Farrar, Strauss & Giroux and the American Scandinavian Foundation, 1975. ix+214p. bibliog.

An attractively illustrated volume with a reasonable amount of text. After two introductory chapters, it looks separately at ceramics, wood and furniture, glass and crystal, textiles, jewellery and metals, and 'trolls, mobiles, et cetera'. The chapters are generally divided country-by-country and Finland is well represented.

619 **Scandinavian domestic design.**
Edited by Erik Zahle. London: Methuen, 1963. 300p.

The chapter on Finland is by Benedict Zilliacus and although it concentrates on the post-Second World War period, particularly the 1950s, it looks also at the traditions of design established from the end of the 19th century. This excellent survey of Finnish design places in context the numerous illustrations of Finnish work which appear with other Scandinavian designs in the main body of the book. Biographies are provided of the artists whose work is illustrated.

Finland creates: the inter-relationship of land and design in Finland.
See item no. 583.

Architecture

620 **800 years of Finnish architecture.**
Sir James M. Richards. Newton Abbot, England: David & Charles, 1978. 191p. map. bibliog.

This admirable and judiciously balanced survey of Finnish architecture supersedes the author's *A guide to Finnish architecture* (London: Evelyn; New York: Praeger, 1967. 112p.). The short, annotated bibliography is mostly of works in English.

621 **Finnish architecture.**
Nils Erik Wickberg. Helsinki: Otava, 1959. reprinted 1962. 242p. map.

An impressive survey of Finnish architecture, starting in mediaeval times but devoting particular attention to the national trends at the beginning of the 20th century and to modern architecture from the 1930s to the 1950s. Rather a brief text but excellent black-and-white illustrations.

622 **Modern architecture.**
Asko Salokorpi. London: Weidenfeld & Nicolson, 1970. 56+64p.

A concise account of Finnish architecture in the 20th century, with well-chosen illustrations and a good introduction and notes on the buildings depicted.

623 **Finnish architecture today.**
Maima Norri. *Look at Finland*, no. 3 (1978), p. 4-11.
Considers especially the architecture of the 1970s and sets it in its Finnish and international context. With illustrations.

624 **Scandinavian architecture: buildings and society in Denmark, Finland, Norway, and Sweden from the Iron Age until today.**
Thomas Paulsson. London: Leonard Hill, 1958. xvi+256p. map.
Aims to provide a handbook for the person interested in architecture and for the person interested in Scandinavia in general. Arranged chiefly by period. Sets Finland in its Scandinavian perspective, perhaps a little too briefly.

625 **Suomen vanhat linnat. The castles of Finland.**
Vesa Mäkinen. Porvoo, Finland: Werner Söderström, 1975. 192p. maps. bibliog.
This combined picture- and guide-book imparts a great deal of information about ancient fortifications in Finland, the mediaeval castles (including that of Viipuri, now in the Soviet Union), and fortified manor houses. The text itself is in Finnish only but there is an English 'Commentary on the contents' on p. 185-88 and the captions to the fine colour illustrations and castle plans also appear in English.

626 **Living historical monuments.**
C. J. Gardberg. *Look at Finland*, no. 3 (1976), p. 28-35.
An expert's account, for the general reader, of restoration work on the castles of Turku, Olavinlinna and Hämeenlinna as well as shorter notes on other restored buildings.

627 **Viapori - historical monument and future arts centre.**
Lea Venkula-Vauraste. *Look at Finland*, no. 3-4 (1977), p. 2-9.
Agreeable pictures of the magnificent fortress of Sveaborg (Viapori, or Suomenlinna), built off Helsinki in the latter half of the 18th century. After many years of military occupation it is now being reduced to an arts centre.

628 **Kauneimmat kirkkomme: suomalaista kirkkoarkkitehtuuria keskiajalta nykypäivään. Finlands vackraste kyrkor: finska kyrkoarkitektur från medeltiden till våra dagar. Die schönsten Kirchen Finnlands: finnische Kirchenarchitektur von Mittelalter bis zur Gegenwart. Finland's most beautiful churches: Finnish church architecture from the Middle Ages up to the present day.**

Edited by Antero Sinisalo, Henrik Lilius, photographs by Per-Olof Welin. Jyväskylä, Finland: Gummerus, 1970. 4th rev. ed. 198p. bibliog.

Pictures (some in colour) with captions in Finnish, Swedish, German and English. The English introduction is somewhat abridged and the notes on the architectural history of the churches depicted appear only in Finnish.

629 **Keskiajan kivikirkot. Finlands medeltida stenkyrkor. The medieval stone churches of Finland.**

Esa Santakari. Helsinki: Otava, 1979. 175p. map. bibliog.

Seventy-five mediaeval stone churches and fifteen stone sacristies have survived in Finland. This book provides fine black-and-white photographs with an introduction (abridged in English) and picture captions in English as well as in Finnish and Swedish. It gives a good impression of the development and character of mediaeval church building in Finland.

630 **Kansanrakentajien puukirkot. Allmogemästarnas träkyrkor. The wooden churches of Finland.**

Esa Santakari. Helsinki: Otava, 1977. 151p.

Constitutes a useful introduction to an important form of Finnish wooden architecture. The Swedish and English introductions are much abridged from the Finnish. Very good black-and-white photographs, with captions in Finnish, Swedish and English.

631 **Towns built from tar: old seaports of western Finland.**

J. M. Richards. *Country Life*, vol. 164, no. 4,228 (20 July 1978), p. 178, 180.

Describes and illustrates some of the wooden buildings of the towns on the Gulf of Bothnia, whose prosperity was founded on the trade in tar. Also comments on the revival of interest in wooden town buildings in Finland.

632 **Talonpoikaistalot - talonpoikaisarkkitehtuurin katoavaa kauneutta. Bondgårdar - bondarkitekturens försvinnande skönhet. Peasant houses - the vanishing beauty of peasant architecture.**

Markus Leppo. Porvoo, Finland: Werner Söderström, 1973. 168p.

Depicts mostly exteriors, though there are a few interiors as well, of wooden peasant houses in southern Ostrobothnia. Mainly black-and-white photographs, but some in colour. Includes interviews with builders and owners. Text and introduction in Finnish, Swedish and English.

633 **New housing in Finland.**
Hans-J. Becker, Wolfram Schlote. London: Tiranti, 1964. 2nd ed. 184p. maps.

This is a report on planning and housing in Finland, describing the process of regional planning, town planning, and estate planning, as well as housing, with examples from the 1950s to the early 1960s. Numerous good illustrations and plans. The text and picture captions are in English and German.

634 **Conservation in action: Finland's historic mill town.**
Marcus Binney. *Country Life*, vol. 165, no. 4,270 (10 May 1979), p. 1444-45.

Describes the history of the mills in Tampere and notes the failure to preserve the historic industrial buildings on the Tammerkoski.

635 **Tapiola: the image and the reality.**
Peter N. Grimshaw. *Town and Country Planning*, vol. 44, no. 6 (June 1976), p. 315-21.

Describes briefly the history and development of the much-visited Tapiola garden city near Helsinki. Considers the town to be 'one of the most pleasant and successful communities created by private, or public, funds'.

636 **Building a new town: Finland's new garden city Tapiola.**
Heikki von Hertzen, Paul D. Spreiregen. Cambridge, Massachusetts; London: MIT Press, 1971. xi+234p. maps.

Contains some interesting material on town planning in Finland as well as a history of the financing, planning, building and operation of Tapiola, in which von Hertzen was the prime mover. Numerous illustrations and plans.

637 **Arquitectura finlandesa en Otaniemi: Alvar Aalto, Heikki Siren, Reima Pietilä.** (Finnish architecture at Otaniemi.)
Maria Lluïsa Borràs. Barcelona, Spain: Ediciones Polígrafa, 1967. 60+CXII+8p.

Photographs (black-and-white and colour) of the buildings of the University of Technology at Otaniemi near Helsinki, with a commentary in Spanish, English, French and German.

638 **Finlandia.**
Architects' Journal, vol. 169, no. 18 (2 May 1979), p. 899-907.

Examines and describes three Finnish buildings (a savings bank, an artists' village and a church), stressing their craftsmanship and consistency in quality of design.

639 **Alvar Aalto.**
London: Academy Editions, 1978. 128p. bibliog. (Architectural Monographs, 4).

Alvar Aalto (1898-1976) is very much the hero-figure of modern Finnish architecture. This is a good introduction to his architecture, containing three essays on different aspects of his work and its background, descriptions of some of his important buildings, and a select bibliography.

640 **Alvar Aalto: das Gesamtwerk. L'oeuvre complète. The complete work.**
Edited by Karl Fleig. Zürich: Editions d'Architecture Artemis, 1970-78. 3 vols.

A subjective impression of Aalto's work with the material for the first two volumes selected by the architect himself. Numerous excellent illustrations and plans. Text in German, French and English.

641 **Alvar Aalto: sketches.**
Edited by Göran Schildt. Cambridge, Massachusetts; London: MIT Press, 1978. ix+172p.

Reprints a number of short articles by Aalto about various aspects of architecture. The book is illustrated with some of Aalto's sketches of natural and architectural subjects.

642 **Alvar Aalto synopsis: painting, architecture, sculpture. Malerei, Architektur, Skulptur. Peinture, architecture, sculpture.**
Basel, Switzerland; Stuttgart, GFR: Birkhäuser Verlag, 1970. 240p. bibliog. (Swiss Federal Institute of Technology, Zürich. History and Theory of Architecture, 12).

The main body of the book consists of excellent reproductions of sketches, plans, sculptures, furniture and paintings by Aalto (some in colour) and of photographs of buildings he designed. There are also extracts from his writings, biographical information, a brief essay by Werner M. Moser entitled 'A survey of the work of Alvar Aalto', a chronological list of works (1918-70), and an extensive classified 'Bibliography 1918-1970', compiled by Leonardo Mosso (p. 209-33). The text is in English, French and German.

643 **Alvar Aalto and the international style.**
Paul David Pearson. New York: Whitney Library of Design, 1978. 240p. bibliog.

An extensive monograph on Aalto's life, ideas and work, emphasizing his role as a master of the modern movement, but ceasing detailed examination of Aalto in 1949. With a long selected bibliography.

644 **Alvar Aalto.**
Edited by Karl Fleig. London: Thames & Hudson, 1975. 207p.

Divided thematically (e.g. urban design, theatres and cultural buildings, family houses, furniture), this book provides very good illustrations and plans to accompany the descriptions of the buildings, etc. It is based on *Alvar Aalto: das Gesamtwerk. L'oeuvre complète. The complete work* (q.v.), which was authorized by the architect himself.

645 **Alvar Aalto.**
Frederick Gutheim. London: Mayflower; New York: Braziller, 1960. 128p. bibliog. (The Masters of World Architecture Series).

A longish introduction on the man and the architecture, setting the latter in its European context. Illustrations of buildings and plans.

646 **Alvar Aalto.**
George Baird, Yukio Futagawa. London: Thames & Hudson, 1970. 130p. bibliog. (Masters of Modern Architecture).

Plans, photographs and notes about a number of Aalto's buildings, with an introduction and a biographical sketch.

647 **Alvar Aalto: a bibliography.**
William C. Miller. Monticello, Illinois: Council of Planning Librarians, 1976. 51p. (Exchange Bibliography, 1190).

Contains: an introduction on Aalto; sections on publications by him (in chronological order); books and monographs solely by him; material on him in works on Finnish art and architecture, and in general works; periodical articles on him and his architecture (this section in chronological order). Unannotated; no index.

648 **Alvar Aalto and the written word.**
Pekka Suhonen. *Books from Finland*, vol. X, nos. 1 and 2 (1976), p. 3-6.

A review article of books about Aalto, commenting that no biography existed which attempted to bring together and assess the full scope of his work as architect, artist, sculptor and man of ideas.

649 **Carl Ludvig Engel.**
Nils Erik Wikberg. Helsinki: City of Helsinki, 1973. [76]p.

Carl Ludvig Engel (1778-1840) was the architect who created the new centre of Helsinki after the city had become Finland's new capital in 1819. This short but excellent study was originally produced in a fuller form for an exhibition about Engel in Berlin in 1970. It concentrates on Engel's work in Helsinki. Fine illustrations (mostly black-and-white) of plans and buildings.

650 **Carl Ludwig Engel: builder of Helsinki.**
Valdemar Melanko. *Look at Finland*, no. 5 (1971), p. 10-15.

A short, illustrated article on the architect who, with Johan Albrekt Ehrenström (the creator of the Helsinki town plan), produced the city 'as a work of art'.

651 **Eliel Saarinen: Finnish-American architect and educator.**
Albert Christ-Janer. Chicago: University of Chicago Press, 1979. rev. ed. xviii+169p. bibliog.

A biography of Eliel Saarinen (1873-1950) presenting a representative group of his buildings, both in Finland and elsewhere. Excellent photographs and extensive bibliography.

652 **Kaija & Heikki Siren: architects, Architekten, architectes.**
Edited by Erik Bruun, Sara Popovits. Stuttgart, GFR: Karl Krämer; Helsinki: Otava, 1978. 2nd. ed. 240p. bibliog.

Illustrations and plans of the work of two modern Finnish architects, from the period 1950-76, starting with the Helsinki University of Technology at Otaniemi and finishing with the Brucknerhaus concert hall in Linz. Text in English, German and French.

653 **Brothers in rock.**
Juha Tanttu. *Look at Finland*, no. 4-5 (1977), p. 10-17.

One of the most popular calls of the tourist buses in Helsinki is the church in Temppeliaukio, cut out of the rock to the design of Timo and Tuomo Suomalainen - the 'brothers in rock' - whose work, particularly the church, is described and illustrated for the general reader in this article.

Helsinki. Helsingfors. Arkkitehtuuriopas. Arkitektur guide. Architectural guide.
See item no. 95.

Music and Dance

Music

654 **Musica Fennica.**
Timo Mäkinen, Seppo Nummi. Helsinki: Otava, 1965. 139p.
Attempts to give a résumé of Finnish music from mediaeval times to the present day, with a concluding chapter on 'The performing arts in Finnish music, and festivals of music'. Lacks an index.

655 **Suomalaista musiikkia. Finnish music. Suomalainen orkesterimusiikki, orkesterisäestyksellinen vokaalimusiikki, oopperamusiikki, balettimusiikki. Finnish orchestral works, vocal works with orchestra, operas, ballets.**
Helsinki: Luovan Säveltaiteen Edistämissäätiö, Foundation for the Promotion of Finnish Music, 1973. 282p.
A list in Finnish and English of orchestral compositions by Finnish composers from Erik Tulindberg (1761-1814) to the present, with notes on each composer. Arranged alphabetically by composer, the book gives details of opus numbers, titles of compositions, year of composition, time of performance, number of performers required, publisher or where to obtain scores and texts, names of writers of texts accompanying compositions, and year and place of first performance, if known.

656 **The music of Finland.**
Denby Richards. London: Evelyn, 1968. viii+120p.
Written as background information for the 'interested music-lover'. Concentrates on modern Finnish composers but also mentions artists and orchestras. The appendix lists the works of selected contemporary composers.

657 **Finland's composers: short historical outline.**
Jarmo Sermilä. Helsinki: Ministry for Foreign Affairs, 1976. 25p.

Brief notes on Finnish composers from Erik Tulindberg (1761-1814) and Bernhard Henrik Crusell (1775-1838) to the avant-gardists of the present.

658 **Composers of Finland.**
Edited by Tauno Karila. Helsinki: Suomen Säveltäjät, 1965. 108p.

A brief introduction on the history of Finnish music and on the work of the Association of Finnish Composers (the publisher) is followed by short biographies of seventy-seven composers active in the 20th century. Each biography is supplemented by a portrait and a list of works.

659 **Sibelius and the music of Finland.**
Veikko Helasvuo. Helsinki: Otava, 1961. 3rd rev. ed. 101p.

A popular survey, concentrating less on Sibelius than on 19th and 20th century Finnish composers, Finnish artists abroad, and various other aspects of Finnish music from musicology to military bands.

660 **Sibelius. Volume I. 1865-1905.**
Erik Tawaststjerna, translated by Robert Layton. London: Faber & Faber, 1976. xv+316p. bibliog.

Jean Sibelius (1865-1957) has dominated Finnish music. Professor Tawaststjerna's biography - still incomplete - is a monumental work both on the man and on the composer and his music. This translation by Robert Layton (who wrote the biography *Sibelius*, q.v.), is an abridged version of volumes 1 and 2 of the original, with revisions by the author. It has been acclaimed as a masterly combination of scholarship and warmth. The book contains musical examples and has an excellent index.

661 **Sibelius: a personal portrait.**
Santeri Levas. London: Dent, 1972. xxiii+165p.

A shortened version of a Finnish original by Sibelius's secretary. A short biographical introduction is followed by the author's impressions and an indication of the views of the composer. Contains only a brief discussion of the main musical works. List of works and a selected discography. Described by Blum in *Jean Sibelius: an international bibliography* (q.v.) as a basic contribution.

662 **Sibelius.**
Robert Layton. London: Dent, 1978. rev. ed. xi+210p. bibliog. (The Master Musicians Series).

Relatively little biographical information but much on the works, which are often analysed in some detail, with musical examples. Catalogue of works and a considerable bibliography.

663 **Sibelius and his world.**
Robert Layton. London: Thames & Hudson, 1970. 120p.

Essentially a picture book though with a good biographical text. The illustrations are taken from a pictorial biography of Sibelius by Ilkka Oramo.

664 **Jean Sibelius.**
Harold E. Johnson. London: Faber & Faber, 1960. 255p. bibliog.

Described by Blum in *Jean Sibelius: an international bibliography* (q.v.) as an attempt at an objective biography, using libraries and archives and not interviewing the subject. Contains a 'Complete list of compositions and arrangements'.

665 **Jean Sibelius: his life and personality.**
Karl Ekman. New York: Knopf, 1938. [xiv]+298+xp.

Written in close collaboration with the composer, this sympathetic study is much more on the 'life and personality' than on the analysis of the music. It concludes with a list of Sibelius's works (to 1929).

666 **Sibelius.**
Cecil Gray. London: Oxford University Press, 1934. reprinted, 1945. 2nd ed. [vii]+224p.

Much more on the music than on the man.

667 **Sibelius: the symphonies.**
Cecil Gray. London: Oxford University Press, 1935. 77p. (The Musical Pilgrim).

Describes the seven symphonies, with musical examples. The book complements the shorter survey of the symphonies in the author's *Sibelius* (see the previous item).

668 **Sibelius: a symposium.**
Edited by Gerald Abraham. London: Lindsay Drummond, 1947. 188+[ii]+28p. bibliog. (Music of the Masters).

669 **The music of Sibelius.**
Edited by Gerald Abraham. New York: Norton, 1947. Reprinted, New York: Da Capo Press, 1975. [iv]+218p. bibliog. (Da Capo Press Music Reprint Series).

This book and the previous entry are the same work with different titles. Chapters by various authors on the man, the different types of music composed by Sibelius, special characteristics of his style, together with a chronology, bibliography, indexed list of works and twenty-eight pages of musical examples. Considered authoritative on the music.

670 **Jean Sibelius: an international bibliography on the occasion of the centennial celebrations, 1965.**
Fred Blum. Detroit, Michigan: Information Service, 1965. xxi+114p. (Detroit Studies in Music Bibliography, 8).

Over 1,400 entries: books and journal articles, which are classified and have references to translations and reviews. The introduction provides a critical appreciation of the main works cited.

671 **Finnish folk music.**
Paavo Helistö. Helsinki: Foundation for the Promotion of Finnish Music, Finnish Music Information Centre, 1973. 30p.

A pamphlet describing the instruments used for Finnish folk music, the flourishing state of folk music, and composers and festivals, as well as listing folk music archives, publications, and a selection of recorded Finnish folk music.

672 **Finnish jazz: history, musicians, discography.**
Edited by Åke Granholm. Helsinki: Foundation for the Promotion of Finnish Music, Finnish Music Information Centre. 1974. 39p.

A short history of Finnish jazz, with biographical notes of musicians and a discography.

673 **Opera in Finland.**
Erkki Arni. *Records and Recording*, vol. 22, no. 9 (June 1979), p. 34-35.

A very brief history of opera in Finland and of the Finnish National Opera, written to mark the performances of two modern Finnish operas in London in June 1979.

674 **Literature into libretto.**
Erkki Arni. *Books from Finland*, vol. XI, no. 1 (1977), p. 85-90.

Describes four modern Finnish operas: Leevi Madetoja's *Pohjalaisia* (The Ostrobothnians), based on a play by Artturi Järviluoma; Aarre Merikanto's *Juha*, based on a novel by Juhani Aho; Aulis Sallinen's *Ratsumies* (The horseman, q.v.), libretto by Paavo Haavikko; and Joonas Kokkonen's *Viimeiset kiusaukset* (The last temptations), libretto by Lauri Kokkonen.

675 **Martti Talvela: the bass of the century.**
Seppo Heikinheimo. *Look at Finland*, no. 3 (1978), p. 32-37.

Martti Talvela is internationally acclaimed as a great singer. This article for the general reader examines the nature and reasons for that acclaim and also describes Talvela's work as artistic director of the Savonlinna Opera Festival. Good illustrations.

***The horseman*: the libretto of the opera composed by Aulis Sallinen.**
See item no. 542.

Dance

676 **Old Finnish folk dances.**
Edited by Orvokki Komulainen. Helsinki: Suomalaisen kansantanssin ystävät, 1973. 43p.

A short introduction on the background, music and costumes, is followed by a collection of folk dances with music and explanations of steps, formations and figures: dances in circle formation; dances in two lines; dances in square formation; and dances in other formations.

677 **Fifty years of Finnish ballet.**
Lea Venkula-Vauraste. *Look at Finland*, no. 4-5 (1972), p. 34-37.

A short, popular note of the history, repertoire and dancers of the Finnish National Opera Ballet.

Theatre and Film

Theatre

678 **Finnish theatre: a northern part of world theatre.**
Maija Savutie. Helsinki: Otava, 1980. 64p.

Finland has forty-two regular, professional theatres, a high figure in relation to the size of the population. Illustrated with pictures of theatres, writers and productions, this little book attempts to pick out the features of Finnish theatre which are of interest abroad. Concludes that, although the recession and administrative preoccupations are causing problems at present, the general picture is not one of stagnation.

679 **Finnish theatre today.**
Edited by Katri Veltheim, Ilona Tainio. Helsinki: Finnish Centre of the International Theatre Institute (ITI), 1971. 71p.

Short sections on theatre history, the administration of the Finnish theatre, modern playwrights, active producers, 'towards a new theatre', and the Finnish theatre's connections abroad. Not superseded in all respects by the previous entry.

680 **Suomen Kansallisteatteri. The Finnish National Theatre.**
Edited by Ritva Heikkilä. Porvoo, Finland: Werner Söderström, 1962. 2nd rev. ed. 279p.

First published to mark the ninetieth anniversary of the foundation of the Finnish National Theatre and revised for the centenary. Very brief introduction; numerous illustrations of actors and productions. Lists of the company's tours, visiting companies, and the most popular productions. Texts in Finnish and English.

681 **News from the Finnish Theatre. Nouvelles du théâtre finlandais.**
Helsinki: Finnish Centre of the ITI, Centre finlandais de l'IIT, 1958- . semi-annual.

Contents in English and French. Articles about theatres, playwrights, productions (drama and opera), tours and festivals. Photographs of productions. Has had various changes of title.

Film

682 **Finnish cinema.**
Peter Cowie. London: Tantivy Press; South Brunswick, New York: A. S. Barnes; Helsinki: Finnish Film Foundation, 1976. 128p. bibliog.

Considers the development and history of the Finnish cinema, identifying particular themes and examining modern films more closely. 'Filmographies' (biographical notes of notable directors) and a very brief bibliography.

683 **Cinema in Finland: an introduction.**
Edited by Jim Hillier. London: British Film Institute, 1975. vii+67p.

Designed to be an introduction to the traditions, history and achievements of the Finnish cinema in general and as a guide to films which the Finnish Film Archive can provide for non-commercial screenings. Has a chronology, and also notes on directors, credits and commentary of the available films.

684 **Finland filmland. Facts about film in Finland.**
Helsinki: Suomen elokuvasäätiö (Finnish Film Foundation), 1970- . irregular.

Contains articles on the history of film in Finland as well as information about new films, producers and directors. Combines two periodicals: *Finland-filmland* (started 1970) and *Facts About Film Finland* (started 1971).

Sports and Recreation

Sports

685 **Physical education and sports in Finland.**
Porvoo, Finland: Werner Söderström, 1979. 3rd ed. 126p. (The Finnish Society for Research in Sports and Physical Education Publication, 65).

This handy introduction includes physical education and the training of PE instructors, the organization of sport, and sports facilities.

686 **Sports organizations: a unique part of Finnish society.**
Paavo Seppänen. *Look at Finland*, no. 4-5 (1976), p. 8-17.

A history of the Finnish sports organizations: SVUL (Finnish Central Sports Federation), CIF (Swedish-speaking Central Sports Federation) and TUL (Workers' Sports Federation). Although bedevilled by political differences, the sports organizations have succeeded in promoting sport in Finland to a high degree and have contributed to success abroad.

687 **Next target Moscow.**
Antero Raevuori. *Look at Finland*, no. 4-5 (1976), p. 18-25.

One of the best-known contemporary Finns is Lasse Virén, the Olympic champion runner, described and depicted in this article. There were to be no medals for Virén at the 1980 Moscow Olympics.

688 **The myth and the man.**
Erkki Savolainen. *Look at Finland*, no. 1 (1974), p. 50-54.
An article to mark the death of Paavo Nurmi (1897-1973), the famous 'Flying Finn' who 'ran Finland on the world map' in the 1920s.

689 **Finnish baseball: a game of skill and speed.**
Antero Raevuori. *Look at Finland*, no. 5 (1977), p. 54-59.
Devised by Professor Lauri Pihkala, inspired by American baseball but very different in character, Finnish baseball is a major sport with some 100,000 active players and a keen following.

690 **A rally driver at home.**
Antero Raevuori. *Look at Finland*, no. 3 (1978), p. 42-47.
Finnish rally drivers have attained an international reputation and perhaps none more than Timo Mäkinen, whose career and home life are described here.

Sauna

691 **Let's have a sauna.**
Marjatta Herva, illustrated by Henrik Tikkanen. Helsinki: Sauna-Seura (Finnish Sauna Society), 1978. 22p.
A brief explanation of the history and workings of the sauna, the Finnish steam bath, whose popularity has spread widely in recent years. Recommends what to do and not to do as regards sauna. Nice drawings by Henrik Tikkanen.

692 **The sauna book.**
Tom Johnson, Tim Miller. New York: Harper & Row, 1977. [x]+197p.
Tells how to take a sauna and make a sauna, with details of saunas on the market.

693 **The international handbook of Finnish sauna.**
Allan Konya, Alewyn Burger. London: Architectural Press, 1973. 176p.
Describes what a sauna is, but concentrates on how a sauna is built, covering all aspects of materials, construction and stoves. Includes a list of manufacturers, distributors and agents. Very clear and thorough presentation.

694 **Suomalainen/Finnish/Finnische Sauna/finlandaise.**
A. Reinikainen. MTR-Studio, 1977. 120p.
A practical guide to the use and construction of saunas with a list of relevant firms.

695 **Sauna: the Finnish bath.**
H. J. Viherjuuri. Brattleboro, Vermont: Stephen Greene Press, 1972. viii+89p.

On the history, preparation and use of the sauna, its effects, and how to build a sauna. Short but reliable.

696 **The Finnish sauna: peace of mind, body and soul.**
John O. Virtanen. Portland, Oregon: Continental Publishing House, 1974. [vi]+232p. maps.

A personal account of the history and practice of the sauna; describes how to make a sauna.

697 **Sauna studies: papers read at the VI International Sauna Congress in Helsinki on August 15-17, 1974.**
Helsinki: Finnish Sauna Society, 1976. 301p.

Includes a number of medical sauna studies, among them a somewhat discouragingly entitled paper on 'Sudden death during and after sauna bath'. Also sections on planning and building the sauna, sauna technology and sauna and sports.

Food and drink

698 **Finnish food for your table.**
Peggie Benton. Oxford, England: Cassirer, 1960. [viii]+116p.

A considerable number of recipes, with some comments on Finnish eating habits. Starts, appropriately, with soups, and finishes with special dishes for feast days. Lacks illustrations of the dishes.

699 **Kalakukko, pea soup and Carelian pastries.**
Mari Blåfield. *Look at Finland*, no. 3 (1973), p. 45-51.

A note on Finnish food, particularly what ordinary Finns eat; the illustrations are not, however, of everyday dishes. *Kalakukko*, mentioned in the title, is a fish pasty originating in eastern Finland.

700 **Natural cooking the Finnish way.**
Ulla Käkönen. New York: Quadrangle, the New York Times Book Company, 1974. [xiii]+209p.

An extensive, practical cookery book, comprising an excellent range of recipes.

701 **The Finnish cook book.**
Beatrice A. Ojakangas. New York: Crown, 1979. 13th printing. 250p. bibliog. (International Cook Book Series).

A wide-ranging book of Finnish recipes, adapted for American use.

702 **From table to palate.**
Sinikka Salokorpi. *Look at Finland*, no. 5 (1974), p. 36-43.
Describes various Finnish comestibles and beverages from rye bread to liqueurs.

703 **Finlandia gastronomica: a guide to Finnish food.**
Matti Viherjuuri, Anna-Maija Tanttu, Juha Tanttu. Helsinki: Otava, 1978. 3rd ed. 62p. (Finderland for Foodlovers).
Not just a recipe book but also contains plenty of information about formal and less-formal eating and drinking habits. Attractive illustrations.

Libraries, Archives, Museums and Art Galleries

Libraries

704 **Libraries in Scandinavia.**

K. C. Harrison. London: Deutsch, 1969. 2nd ed. entirely rev. and rewritten. 288p. bibliog.

Book IV: Finland, p. 213-47, contains chapters on: academic and research libraries in Finland; library law and state aid; education and organization for Finnish librarianship; public libraries in Finland. Now inevitably dated, it remains useful background reading.

705 **Finland.**

London: Libraries Department, British Council, 1977. 12p. bibliog. (Library and Books Profile).

One of a series of profiles prepared by the British Council on libraries, publishing and the book trade. Provides a handy survey of the Finnish scene, with appropriate statistics. Copies may be obtained from: Libraries Department, British Council, 10 Spring Gardens, London SW1A 2BN. A new edition is in preparation.

706 **The Finnish library scene.**

New Library World, vol. 76, no. 903 (Sept. 1975), p. 179-87, 189.

Comprises six short articles by Finnish specialists which together make up an account of libraries in Finland. The articles cover: Finnish library buildings; trends in scientific and technical information in Finland; public libraries in Finland; developing research libraries in Finland; library training in Finland; and the bookmobile service in Finland.

707 **Abstract of the report submitted by the 1973 Library Committee.**
Helsinki: Government Printing Centre, 1975. 32p. (Committee Report 1975: 110).

The report concerns plans for the development of the Finnish public library system. Discussions about it are continuing.

708 **A unified approach to science information and research libraries in Finland.**
Esko Häkli. *Unesco Bulletin for Libraries*, vol. XXVIII, no. 5 (Sept.-Oct. 1974), p. 245-48.

Describes the Finnish Council for Scientific Information and Research Libraries (TINFO), its establishment, working principles, and precursors.

709 **Suomen tieteellisten kirjastojen opas. Guide to research libraries and information services in Finland.**
Matti Liinamaa, Marjatta Heikkilä. Helsinki: Suomen tieteellinen kirjastoseura, 1976. 5th rev. and enl. ed. IX+149p. bibliog.

This is an alphabetical list of Finnish research libraries and information services, giving basic information about addresses, hours of opening, collections, etc. With a UDC index and an alphabetical subject index. An alphabetical index of libraries is provided in Swedish and English and the work is not difficult to use for readers with no knowledge of Finnish.

710 **Helsinki University Library.**
Esko Häkli. *Books from Finland*, vol. XI, no. 1 (1977), p. 105-11.

An illustrated account of the history, services and collections of the national library of Finland, by its Chief Librarian.

711 **Helsinki University Library: a short history.**
Henrik Grönroos, Kaija Myllyniemi. Helsinki: Helsinki University Library, 1965. 2nd rev. ed. 36p. bibliog.

On the history of the library, its premises, departments and collections. Older than the previous entry but fuller.

712 **Kirjastolehti.** (Library Journal.)
Helsinki: Suomen Kirjastoseura, 1908- . monthly.

The journal of the Finnish Library Association (Suomen Kirjastoseura), which was entitled *Kansanvalistus ja kirjastolehti* (Public Education and Library Journal) from 1921 to 1947. Publishes articles and statistics on librarianship and libraries, with an emphasis on public libraries. Abstracts of the articles appear in English. *Kirjastolehti* contains two supplements. *Arvosteleva kirjaluettelo* (Critical Book List) (q.v.), and *Esittelevä elokuvaluettelo* (Descriptive List of Films), which is an annotated list of films, Finnish and foreign.

713 **Signum.**
Helsinki: Suomen Kirjallisuuspalvelun Seura & Suomen tieteellinen kirjastoseura, 1968- . 10 issues per year.
Published by the Finnish Association for Documentation and the Association of Scientific Libraries in Finland. Contains articles and notices about information science and about specialized aspects of the work of research libraries. The articles have abstracts in English.

Archives

714 **Suomen arkistojen opas. Arkiven i Finland: en handledning. Guide to archives repositories in Finland.**
Helsinki: National Archives of Finland, 1975. iii+83p. bibliog. (Valtionarkiston julkaisuja. Publikationer av riksarkivet. Publications of the National Archives of Finland, 6).
This short guide provides systematic notes (in Finnish) on the scope and facilities of archives in Finland, including collections in libraries and museums, together with remarks on archival organization and access. The list of contents, key to the arrangement, and alphabetical index of archives repositories are given in English and Swedish as well as Finnish.

715 **Guide to the public archives of Finland.**
Helsinki: National Archives, 1980. 50p. map. bibliog.
'The aims of this Guide . . . are to provide foreign scholars with an introduction to the National Archives and the provincial archives as research institutes and to give practical advice about their use to those undertaking research.' The guide outlines the development of archive administration in Finland, the establishment of the National Archives and, later, of the provincial archives; it lists their functions, provides information about their services and facilities and indicates the main type of records to be found in the public archives.

716 **Finland.**
Kent Forster. In: *The new guide to the diplomatic archives of western Europe.* Daniel H. Thomas and Lynn M. Case. Philadelphia: University of Pennsylvania Press, 1975, p. 56-68. bibliog.
A useful short survey of Finnish archives and libraries holding material of foreign policy interest.

717 **Guide to the Military Archives of Finland.**
Edited by Risto Ropponen. Helsinki: Military Archives, 1977. [iv]+56p. bibliog.

This is not simply a practical guide to the holdings of the Military Archives and how to use them; it also includes (on p. 1-9) a most convenient historical outline of the organization of the Finnish defence forces.

Museums and art galleries

718 **Finnish museums.**
Helsinki: Suomen museoliitto, Finnish Museums Association, 1979. 121p. maps. (Suomen museoliiton julkaisuja [Publications of the Finnish Museums Association], 18).

A list of museums, including art galleries, according to place, with an index arranged according to provinces. Brief details include address, opening hours, ownership and direction, scope and size of collections, guides and publications.

719 **National Museum of Finland: guide.**
Helsinki: National Board of Antiquities and Historical Monuments, 1978. 3rd ed. [112]p.

Describes the collections of the museum: Prehistoric Section; Historic Section; Ethnographic Section; Finno-Ugric Collections; and Cabinet of Coins and Medals. Forms a handy short introduction to Finnish prehistory, history and ethnography.

720 **Folk costumes and textiles.**
National Museum of Finland Ethnographic Department. Helsinki: National Museum of Finland. [n.d.] [64]p. map.

Describes the collections of folk costumes, embroidery and weaving in the National Museum. Well-illustrated.

721 **Seurasaari ulkomuseo/open-air museum.**
István Rácz, Niilo Valonen. Helsinki: Otava, 1973. 24+[82]p.

A description of the principal Finnish open air museum at Seurasaari near Helsinki, which is internationally famous as a leading example of its type. There is a summary of the introduction in English and the picture captions are in English and Finnish.

Books and the Media

Book trade

722 **Finland.**

In: *The book trade of the world. Volume I: Europe and international section.* Edited by Sigfred Taubert. Hamburg, GFR: Verlag für Buchmarkt-Forschung; London: Deutsch; New York: Bowker, 1972, p. 170-78. map. bibliog.

Provides a systematic summary of the condition and organization of the book trade and of book production and publishing.

723 **Books from Finland.**

Helsinki: Helsinki University Library, 1967- . quarterly.

Originally published by the Publishers' Association of Finland, *Books from Finland* changed completely in style and content with its change of publisher in 1976. It now contains articles about Finnish literature and translations of creative writing as well as reviews and a selective, annotated bibliography of new publications. *Books from Finland* is the only periodical about Finnish literature in an international language and as such is of considerable value both to those interested in that literature and in Finnish publishing, and also to librarians concerned with the selection of Finnish books.

Finland.
See item no. 705.

The press

724 **The press in Finland.**
Helsinki: Finnish Newspaper Publishers' Association, 1980. [16]p.

A handy, brief statement about the Finnish press, including figures for newspaper circulation in 1979.

725 **In quest of freedom: Finland's press, 1771-1971.**
Torsten Steinby. Helsinki: Government Printing Centre, 1972. 163p.

Steinby, a journalist, gives a short account of the historical development of the newspaper press in Finland. The book ends with a list of Finnish daily newspapers in 1971, giving *inter alia* party affiliations and circulation.

726 **Finnish press laws.**
Helsinki: Ministry for Foreign Affairs, Press and Culture Bureau, 1976. 3+54f.

This is a translation of the most important laws relating to the press, showing the provisions for safeguarding the freedom of the press and the constraints which journalists must observe.

Radio and television

727 **Finnish Broadcasting Company YLE 50 1926-1976.**
Helsinki: Yleisradio, 1976. 35p.

An illustrated booklet published to mark the fiftieth anniversary of Yleisradio, the Finnish Broadcasting Company, which has the sole permit for radio broadcasting in the country and most of the air time for television. Describes briefly the history, technical operations, and the orchestra and choirs maintained by the company.

728 **YLE: Finland, Finlande, Finlandia, Finnland, Finlyandiya. Radio & TV 1975.**
Helsinki: Yleisradio, 1975. 24p. bibliog.

Brief multilingual explanations of the activity of Yleisradio. The statistics give figures for 1973. The bibliography lists English-language reports prepared by the company.

729 **Informational mass communication: a collection of essays.** Edited by Kaarle Nordenstreng. Helsinki: Tammi, 1973. 199p. bibliog.

Finnish broadcasting became highly controversial in the 1960s when the proponents of what became known as 'informational programme policy' - among them the authors of these essays - began to propagate left-wing and anti-capitalist opinions in the name of democratization. The views propounded in this book have since sustained setbacks and Finnish broadcasting is now more balanced.

730 **The freedom of expression in radio and television in Finland.** Tore Modeen. *Revue des Droits de l'Homme. Human Rights Journal*, vol. 8, no. 1 (1975), p. 151-64. bibliog.

The author concludes that 'the present situation under which the Government has no possibility to censor radio or TV programs and only the [Finnish Broadcasting] Corporation is entitled to use routine preliminary control of the programs, must be considered satisfactory, particularly since the practice seems to be very liberal and allows a great diversity of opinions to be sent over the air'.

Periodicals and Newspapers

Periodicals

731 **Finsk tidskrift.** (Finnish Review.)
Turku: Föreningen Granskaren, 1876- . 10 issues per year.
This Swedish-language publication on cultural, economic and political topics is the oldest cultural periodical in Scandinavia.

732 **Kanava.** (Channel.)
Helsinki: Yhtyneet Kuvalehdet, 1973- . 9 issues per year.
A periodical in Finnish publishing articles on social, cultural, political and historical topics as well as reviews. It succeeded the older-established *Suomalainen Suomi* (Finnish Finland) and *Aika* (Time).

733 **Kotimaisten sanoma- ja aikakauslehtien hinnasto. Inhemsk tidnings- och tidskriftstaxa.** (Price List of Finnish Newspapers and Periodicals.)
Helsinki: Posti- ja lennätinlaitos, 1971- .
An annual list of newspapers and periodicals, with regularly published supplements. Gives publishers' names and addresses, frequency and subscription rates. Useful for checking the frequency of titles but does not include all Finnish periodicals. Published by the Post and Telegraph Department: previous years had other titles.

734 **Look at Finland.**
Helsinki: Finnish Tourist Board and Ministry for Foreign Affairs, Press Section, 1964- . quarterly.

A well-illustrated periodical intended for foreigners. Articles on various aspects of Finnish life, culture, history and industry, as well as a good deal of tourist information, including a calendar of forthcoming events.

735 **Nya Argus.** (New Argus.)
Helsinki: Nya Argus, 1908- . 16 issues per year.

Originally published as *Argus*, 1908-11, this is a Swedish-language periodical on cultural, social and economic topics.

736 **Scandinavian Review.**
New York: American Scandinavian Foundation, 1913- . quarterly.

Originally published as *American-Scandinavian Review*, 1913-74, volumes 1 to 62. Publishes articles, translations of creative writing, and book and film reviews. Not, of course, confined to Finland.

737 **Suomen kuvalehti.** (Finnish Picture Post.)
Helsinki: Yhtyneet Kuvalehdet, 1916- . weekly.

An illustrated weekly in Finnish which contains news and feature articles on Finnish and world events and issues.

Newspapers

738 **Aamulehti.** (Morning Post.)
Tampere, Finland: Tampereen Kirjapaino, 1882- . daily.

Daily Finnish-language newspaper with a large circulation outside its native Tampere. Supports the Conservative Party (Kokoomus).

739 **Helsingin Sanomat.** (Helsinki News.)
Helsinki: Sanoma, 1890- . daily.

Originally *Päivälehti* (Daily Post), 1890-1904. Has the largest circulation of any Finnish newspaper. A Finnish-language daily, with no party affiliation.

740 **Hufvudstadsbladet.** (News of the Capital.)
Helsinki: Hufvudstadsbladet, 1864- . daily.

Swedish-language newspaper, with the largest circulation of any such paper in the country.

741 **Uusi Suomi.** (New Finland.)
Helsinki: Uusi Suomi, 1847- . daily.

Founded in 1847 as *Suometar*, became *Uusi Suometar* in 1869 and *Uusi Suomi* in 1919. Finnish-language, conservative newspaper.

Encyclopaedias, Yearbooks and Biographical Dictionaries

Encyclopaedias

742 **The power of the word: the popularity of the encyclopaedia in Finland.**
Keijo Kylävaara. *Books from Finland*, vol. XIII, no. 1 (1979), p. 5-7.

In rather more than seventy years, the Finns have shown themselves to be great buyers of encyclopaedias, with a veritable explosion of publishing in the 1970s.

743 **Otavan iso tietosanakirja. Encyclopaedia Fennica.** (Otava's great encyclopaedia.)
Helsinki: Otava, 1960-65. 10 vols.

An extensive traditional encyclopaedia, with some 100,000 entry words. Chiefly by Finnish authors; the longer articles are signed and give short bibliographies. Volume 10 contains a general index of about 90,000 entry words to names, titles, etc., which appear within articles in the main alphabetical sequence of the encyclopaedia. There is also a gazetteer to the maps.

744 **Uusi tietosanakirja.** (New encyclopaedia.)
Helsinki: Tietosanakirja, 1960-66. 24 vols.; Helsinki: Werner Söderström, Tietosanakirja, 1972. 2 supplementary vols.

A traditional alphabetical encyclopaedia, compiled chiefly by Finns; contributors are listed but articles are not signed. Short bibliographies to articles. The index (in volume 24) has about 125,000 entry words.

745 **Facta. 10-osainen tietosanakirja.** (Facta. 10-volume encyclopaedia.)
Helsinki: Tietosanakirja & Werner Söderström, 1969-71. 10 vols.

A traditional encyclopaedia with over 70,000 alphabetically arranged entry words. Contributors are listed and their subject fields given, but articles are not signed and there are few short bibliographies. A supplement volume which also includes indexes, with 300,000 entry words, was published in 1975.

746 **Otavan iso Fokus: kertovasti kuvitettu 8-osainen tietosanakirja.** (Otava's great Fokus: 8-volume encyclopaedia with descriptive illustrations.)
Helsinki: Otava, 1971-75. 8 vols.

This encyclopaedia is based on a Swedish original but was revised for Finnish readers. Volumes 1-7 contain some 50,000 alphabetically arranged articles and about 200 longer articles on broader subjects. Extensive use of illustrations and diagrams is a feature of the work. Volume 8 contains an alphabetical index (some 200,000 entry words) and tables giving a wide variety of information from foreign terms relating to food and drink to national coats of arms; also includes bibliographies by subject. The articles are unsigned but contributors are listed with their subject fields.

747 **Otavan suuri ensyklopedia.** (Otava's great encyclopaedia.)
Helsinki: Otava, 1976- .

A twelve-volume encyclopaedia due to be completed in 1982 (volume 8 was published in 1980). It is based on the French *La grande encyclopêdie Larousse,* but makes extensive use of Finnish collaborators. The first ten volumes are to comprise about 5,000 alphabetically arranged broad articles and the last two volumes are to provide detailed indexes. Numerous excellent illustrations and maps. Articles signed; short bibliographies. Interim indexes are being published to facilitate use of the work. Particularly good on the humanities, this is one of the two 'new generation' of Finnish encyclopaedias, the other being *Spectrum tietokeskus* (see the following entry).

748 **Spectrum tietokeskus: 16-osainen tietosanakirja.** (Spectrum information centre: 16-volume encyclopaedia.)
Helsinki: Werner Söderström, 1976-

This sixteen volume encyclopaedia is due to be completed by 1981: volume 12 (Tal-Uzb) was published in 1980. The work is based on a Dutch model, *Grote Spectrum encyklopedie,* but uses numerous Finnish contributors. The first fourteen volumes are to contain some 9,000 alphabetically arranged broad articles, and the last two will be detailed indexes. Fine illustrations; there are particularly good articles on technical and scientific subjects. The articles are not signed, though contributors are listed. There are no bibliographies. An interim index was published in 1978. This is one of the two 'new generation' of Finnish encyclopaedias, the other being *Otavan suuri ensyklopedia* (see the preceding entry).

749 **Tiedon värikäs maailma: nykyaikainen tietosanakirja.** (The colourful world of knowledge: a modern encyclopaedia.)
Helsinki: Uusi Kirjakerho, 1972-80. 21 vols.

A traditional-style alphabetical encyclopaedia with modern illustrations. Contains a list of Finnish contributors and their subject fields, but articles are not signed. Acknowledgements are made to *Encyclopedia universo* and to the *Visum encyclopaedia.* The work is also produced as *Kodin suuri tietosanakirja* (see the following entry).

750 **Kodin suuri tietosanakirja.** (The great encyclopaedia of the home.)
Helsinki: Weilin & Göös, 1975- .

The same work as *Tiedon värikäs maailma* (preceding entry) in fewer but larger volumes. Still in progress: volume 14 (Tilat-Verr) was published in 1979.

Yearbooks

751 **Mitä - missä - milloin: kansalaisen vuosikirja.** (What - Where - When: the Citizen's Yearbook.)
Helsinki: Otava, 1951- . annual.

An informative annual containing articles and surveys on a wide range of topics on Finland and elsewhere.

752 **Suomen valtiokalenteri. Julkaissut Helsingin yliopisto.** (The Official Yearbook of Finland. Published by Helsinki University.)
Espoo, Finland: Weilin & Göös, 1869- . annual.

This important work lists government departments with their senior officials, as well as local government and the churches; it provides information about political parties, the press, societies and organizations of various types. There is a shorter Swedish version: *Finlands statskalender* (Espoo, Finland: Weilin & Göös, 1810-).

Biographical dictionaries

753 **Kuka kukin on. (Aikalaiskirja.) Who's who in Finland. Henkilötietoja nykypolven suomalaisista.** (Personal information about Finns of the present generation.)
Helsinki: Otava, 1978. 1,156p.

Has entries for about 4,600 living Finns. In the case of certain retired individuals and persons who did not respond to the compilers' questionnaire, reference is made to fuller entries in previous volumes (see *Kuka kukin oli*). A 'Table of English equivalents of some common signs, words and abbreviations' makes it possible to use the work without a knowledge of Finnish.

754 **Vem och vad? Biografisk handbok 1980.** (Who and what? Biographical handbook 1980.)
Edited by Henrik Ekberg. Helsinki: Schildt, 1979. 785p.

The twelfth in a series of biographical reference books about notable living Finns (mainly Swedish Finns). Some 3,000 biographies.

755 **Dictionary of Scandinavian biography.**
Cambridge, England: International Biographical Centre, 1976. 2nd ed. xxviii+497p.

Biographies of over 4,000 living Scandinavians from the five Nordic countries.

756 **Kuka kukin oli. Who was who in Finland. Henkilötietoja 1900-luvulla kuolleista julkisuuden suomalaisista.** (Personal information about Finns in public life who died in the 20th century.)
Helsinki: Otava, 1961. 593p.

Comprises 2,614 biographies of prominent Finns who died after 1 January 1900 and thus includes many persons active in the 19th century. The volumes of *Kuka kukin on* for 1964, 1970 and 1974 may be used to complement both *Kuka kukin oli* and *Kuka kukin on* 1978 (q.v.).

757 **Suomen talouselämän johtajia. Vem är vem i Finlands ekonomiska liv. Who's who in the economic life of Finland.**
Helsinki: Kirjayhtymä, 1977. 335p.

Data on 2,500 managers and directors in Finnish business and industry. Explanation of abbreviations also given in English.

Bibliographies

758 **Finlands bibliografiska litteratur: kommenterad förteckning.** (Finnish bibliographical works: an annotated list).
Henrik Grönroos. Ekenäs, Finland: Ekenäs tryckeri, 1976. 388p.

The aim of this annotated bibliography of Finnish bibliographies is to assist readers in Scandinavia. The inclusion of a brief summary in English has facilitated its use elsewhere - fortunately, since this is the essential Finnish bibliographical reference book. It covers general bibliographies, Finland in foreign writing and foreign countries in Finnish writing, subject bibliographies and bibliographies of individuals. The indexes include Swedish-Finnish and Finnish-Swedish subject indexes. There are over 1,400 entries, cross-referencing is good, and the work is clearly arranged and easy to use. It is a revision of an earlier work: Henrik Grönroos, *Suomen bibliografisen kirjallisuuden opas. Guide des bibliographies finlandaises* (Guide to Finnish bibliographies). (Helsinki: Suomalaisen Kirjallisuuden Seura, 1965. 219p.) which has its table of contents and an abridgement of its introduction translated into French.

759 **Books in English on Finland: a bibliographical list of publications concerning Finland until 1960, including Finnish literature in English translation. Appendix: a selected list of books published from 1961 to 1963 inclusive.**
Hilkka Aaltonen. Turku, Finland: Turku University Library, 1964. 276p. (Publications of Turku University Library, 8).

Contains over 5,000 unannotated entries, comprising both books and periodical articles, arranged in a classified order and with indexes of persons and of anonymous publications. Most items have been examined *de visu*. Very useful.

760 **Finland: sources of information. A selective list of publications 1960-1977.**
Kyllikki Ruokonen, Erkki Vaisto. Helsinki: Helsinki School of Economics Library, 1979. 224p. map. (Helsingin kauppakorkeakoulun julkaisuja [Publications of Helsinki School of Economics], D-39).

Some 4,000 recent references (unannotated), arranged in UDC classified order, to Finnish and foreign material, mainly on economics and business. Most items are in English, except for some bibliographies and journals. Author and subject indexes.

761 **Kaunokirjallisuutemme käännöksiä: bibliografinen luettelo suomenkielisen kaunokirjallisuuden käännöksistä. Livres finnois en traduction: romans, nouvelles, poésies, pièces de théâtre. Guide bibliographique.** (Finnish literature in translation: a bibliographical list of translations of Finnish-language literature. Finnish books in translation: novels, short stories, poetry, plays. Bibliographical guide.)
Sulo Haltsonen, Rauni Puranen. Helsinki: Suomalaisen Kirjallisuuden Seura, 1979. 150p. (Suomi, 122:4).

This is a revised and expanded edition of Haltsonen's bibliography *Suomalaista kaunokirjallisuutta vierailla kielillä...Livres finnois en traduction* (Finnish literature in foreign languages...Finnish books in translation) (Helsinki: Suomalaisen Kirjallisuuden Seura, 1961. 138p.). The new edition adds information about translations from Finnish-language literature for 1961-75 plus some subsequently published works, amounting to about 700 additions to the original work's 1,168 entries. English (p. 10-14) is one of thirty-eight languages represented. The selection of anthologies (p. 114-26) includes material in Western languages; *Kalevala* and folk poetry in English appear on p. 127-28. The table of contents is in Finnish and French.

762 **A select list of books and articles in English, French and German on Finnish politics in the 19th and 20th century.**
Compiled by Martti Julkunen, Anja Lehikoinen. Turku, Finland: Institute of Political History, 1967. 125p. (Institute of Political History, University of Turku Publications, B: 1).

A list, classified by period, of material on politics interpreted in a wide sense. Index of authors. No annotations but very serviceable.

763 **Finland: Books and Publications in Politics, Political History and International Relations.**
Turku, Finland: Institute of Political History, University of Turku 1966- . annual.

A selective list of books, pamphlets and mimeographed works by Finnish authors. Gives brief notes on the authors (often just their academic degrees) and a very brief summary of the subject of each title. A useful guide to new work in its field.

764 **Finland's war years 1939-1945: a list of books and articles concerning the Winter War and the Continuation War, excluding literature in Finnish and Russian.**
Kristina Nyman, preface by K. J. Mikola. Helsinki: Sotahistoriallinen Seura, 1973. XXXII+259p. maps. (Publications of the Society of Military History, 4).

A classified list of books and articles arranged in five sections: 1, the Winter War; 2, the Continuation War; 3, a miscellaneous section of books and articles touching on Finland in the period described but not exclusively about it; 4, Mannerheim; 5, the Åland Islands question (1938-39). Contains 3,410 numbered entries of material published to 1970, and an appendix of about 70 items published in 1970-72. No annotations. Index. The preface by the military historian Colonel K. J. Mikola, 'Finland's wars during World War II (1939-1945)', p. IX-XXXII, is a handy short account of the subject.

765 **Arvosteleva kirjaluettelo.** (Critical Book List.)
Helsinki: Kouluhallitus, 1940-

This is a classified list of new publications which appears also as a supplement to *Kirjastolehti* (Library Journal) (q.v.). There are short annotations or brief reviews (in Finnish) of many titles, intended to facilitate book selection by libraries. *Arvosteleva kirjaluettelo* is a good means, with *Books from Finland* (q.v.), of keeping informed about new Finnish books.

766 **Suomen kirjallisuus. Finlands litteratur. The Finnish National Bibliography.**
Helsinki: Helsinki University Library, 1974- . monthly.

This is the currently published Finnish national bibliography. There is an annual cumulation: *Suomen kirjallisuus: vuosiluettelo. Finlands litteratur: årskatalog. The Finnish National Bibliography: Annual Volume.* This bibliography was preceded by *Suomen kirjallisuus* (Finnish bibliography) 1949-1966 (in three-year periods), while 1967-71 is being covered in a five-year period. For bibliographies covering the period to 1948, and for details of their contents, see Henrik Grönroos, *Finlands bibliografiska litteratur* (q.v.) p. 35-44.

767 **Suomen aikakauslehti-indeksi. Index to Finnish Periodicals.**
Turku, Finland: Turun yliopiston kirjasto, 1961- . annual.

This is an index to, at present, about 200 scholarly and popular periodicals. Classified arrangement (with the headings in the list of contents also given in English). Index of authors.

768 **Suomen aikakauslehti-indeksi. 1803-1863. Index to Finnish periodicals.**
Turku, Finland: Turun yliopiston kirjasto, 1974. VII+211p.

An index to forty-six serials published between 1803 and 1863. Classified arrangement (with the headings in the list of contents also given in English). Index of authors.

Index

The index is a single alphabetical sequence of authors (personal and corporate), titles of publications and subjects. Index entries refer both to the main items and to other works mentioned in the notes to each item. Title entries are in italics. Numeration refers to the items as numbered.

Bosi, R. 210
Bosley, K. 514, 526–527, 551–552, 571
Botany 75
history 443
Bow Island 539
Bowman, James Cloyd 516
Branch, H. 571
Branch, M. 452, 472, 513–514, 552
Brandövägen 8 Brandö Tel. 35 569
Britain
relations with Finland 137–139, 143, 167–168, 174
Broad, Charlie Dunbar 561
Broadcasting 579, 727–729
freedom of expression 730
Broadcasting Company, Finnish - YLE 727–730
history 727
Broms, Bengt 290
Brucknerhaus concert hall, Linz 652
Bruun, E. 611, 652
Budget 326
Building a new town: Finland's new garden city Tapiola 636
Building industry 379
Building materials industry 373
future prospects 373
Building technique 104
Buildings 103
farm 106
historic 582, 591
wooden 631–632
Bureus, Andreas 48
Burger, A. 693
Bus timetables 387
Business 13, 66, 93, 360, 362
bibliographies 760
Business training 356
Businessmen 757
Buttons
design 615

C

Cakes 699
Camping 83, 85
Canals
Saimaa 392
Canoeing 86
Car ferries 388
Carelian pastries 699
Carl Ludvig Engel 649
Carlander, G. 94
Carols 532
Carpelan, B. 538–539
Cartography 66
history 54
Castles 625–626
Castrén, K. 285
Censorship 309, 725, 730
Censuses 194, 423
Central Association of Finnish Forest Industries 410
Central bank policy 334
Central Organization of Finnish Trade Unions - SAK 418–419
Central Pension Security Institute 236
Central Sports Federation - SVUL 686
Central Union for Child Welfare 237
Ceramics
design 618
history 605
Chambers of commerce 356
Changes in the social structure of the Swedish-speaking population in Finland, 1950-1970 206
Charts, Historic 54
Chemicals industry 373
future prospects 373
Chemistry
history 444
pharmaceutical 444
Chew, A. F. 161
Child-rearing 199–200
Child welfare in Finland 237
Children
folklore 518
oral tradition 518
welfare 237
Children's lore 518
Children's stories 538–539, 544, 570
Children's writers, Contemporary 505
Chivalry, Orders of 285
Choirs, Broadcasting 727
Christ-Janer, A. 651
Christian League, Finnish - SKL 267
Christmas festivals 111
food 111
songs 532
trees 111
Chronologies
cinema 683
economic events 325
foreign affairs 289
Church and State 223, 227

D

E

F

I

J

K

L

Land
  maps 49, 53
  ownership 402–403
  reclamation 403
  recovery 71
  statistics 48, 423
  surveying 423
  tenure 53
  uplift 71
Land and people of Finland 25
Land use 402
  law 79
  planning 78
Lander, Patricia Slade 232
Landscape of Finland 34
Landscapes 583
Language, Philosophy of 438
Language teaching 356
Languages 100, 104, 145, 203, 207
  maps 49
Lapland 5, 22
Lapp language 213, 449–450
  grammar 496
  map terms 58
  poetry 571
  readers 496
Lapp poets 571
Lappische Chrestomathie mit grammatikalischem Abriss und Wörterverzeichnis 496
Lappish nation: citizens of four countries 212
Lapps 210–211, 213
Lapps 104, 202, 209–215, 449
  art 211, 213
  bibliographies 213
  culture 209–213, 215
  folklore 213
  history 210–211, 213
  life and customs 210–213
  literature 211, 213
  music 211, 213
  political development 215
  religion 211
  Skolt 214
  social structure 213
Lapps in Finland: the population, their livelihood and their culture 209
Lapsuuteni 558
Lapua movement 153, 155–156
Laqueur, W. 316
Lasky, M. J. 317
Läsning för barn 570
Last Finnish war 179
Last grain race 396
Last tall ships: Gustaf Erikson and the Åland sailing fleets 1872-1947 394
Last temptations 674
Latin language 436
Launonen, H. 503
Lauréus, Alexander 587
Lavean tien laki 564
Lávlo vizar biello-cizaš 571
Law 269–273
  administrative 271
  civil 271
  commercial 271
  criminal 271
  Roman 436
Law and lawyers in Finland 270
Law and order 279
Law, Company 362
Law courts 270, 273
Lawrence, G. R. P. 62
Lawyers 269–271
Layton, R. 660, 662–663
League of Nations
  Åland dispute 144
Leather industry 377
Legal education 270
Legal philosophy 438
Legal system 269–270, 273
Legislation 270–273
  industrial 239
  women 199
Lehikoinen, A. 762
Lehtinen, M. 479
Lehtiö, P. 373
Lehtola, E. 506
Lehtosalo, Pirkko-Liisa 592
Leimu, H. 440
Leino, Eino 551–552
Leino, P. 511
Leirintäalueopas 1980. Camping in Finland 85
Leisure 201
  statistics 424–425
Lemola, T. 447
Lenin
  attitude to Finland's independence 141
Leppänen, S. 341
Leppo, M. 97, 609–610, 632
Leprosy 442
Leskinen, J. 17
Let's have a sauna 691
Let's visit Finland 40

M

O

P

Q

R

Raanut - coverlets 600
Rácz, I. 590–595, 721
Radicalism 233
Radio 579, 727–729
freedom of expression 730
Raevuori, A. 687, 689–690
Räikkönen, E. 184
Railway stations 365
Railways 397–399
illustrations 397
statistics 423
timetables 387
Rajala, P. 573
Rally drivers 690
Ramsden, E. 577
Rantala, Olavi 343
Rantala, Onni 261
Rantavaara, I. 499, 550
Rastas, K. 379
Ratsumies 542, 674
Räty, T. 447
Ravila, P. 492
Reality of "Finlandisation": living under the Soviet shadow 314
Rebourcet, Gabriel 551
Recipes 698, 700–701, 703
Rector of Reigi 547
Red Cross services
history 244
Refugees, World War II
resettlement 403
Regional development 231, 330–331
legislation 331
planning 331
Regional government 268
Regional planning 633
Regionalism
political parties 261
Regions, Geographical 66
Register of exporters 357
Reindeer 213
Reindeer husbandry 408
Reinikainen, A. 694
Relander, T. 339
Religion 18–19, 223–227, 229, 752
Religious art 594
Reluctant Europeans: the attitudes of the Nordic countries towards European integration 303
Renaissance art 595
Reparations 291
Report of the Committee on the Position of Women in Finnish Society 199
Report of the Second Parliamentary Defence Committee, Finland 281
Research 432–433, 448
science 447
sociology 439–440
statistics 423–424
Research Group for Comparative Sociology 205–206
Research Institute for Social Security 235
Research libraries 704, 706, 708, 713
directories 709
Restaurants 81, 83–84, 90
Retail trade 378
cooperatives 354–355
Reverse dictionaries 474
Revolutionary ferment in Finland and the origins of the Civil War 1917-1918 146
Revue Internationale d'Histoire Militaire: Edition Finlandaise 282
Rhymes, Children's 518
Richards, D. 656
Richards, Sir James M. 620, 631
Richards, P. 442
Riddles 517
Rights of man 276–277
Riikonen, E. 465
Rintala, M. 153–154, 156, 183, 188, 554
Rintala, P. 559
Riwkin-Brick, A. 38
Road maps 43–45
Roads
statistics 423
Rohde, P. P. 149–150
Roman: the memoirs of Minutus Lausus Manilianus 578
Ropponen, R. 717
Rosén, G. 244
Rosset, R. 34
Roundwood 375
Rubulis, A. 535
Rugs, Ryijy 598, 600–601
history 599
Runeberg, Johan Ludvig 532, 560–561
Ruokonen, K. 760
Rural population 198
Rural settlements
history 55

S

T

U

V

W

Y

Z

Map of Finland

This map shows the more important towns and other features.

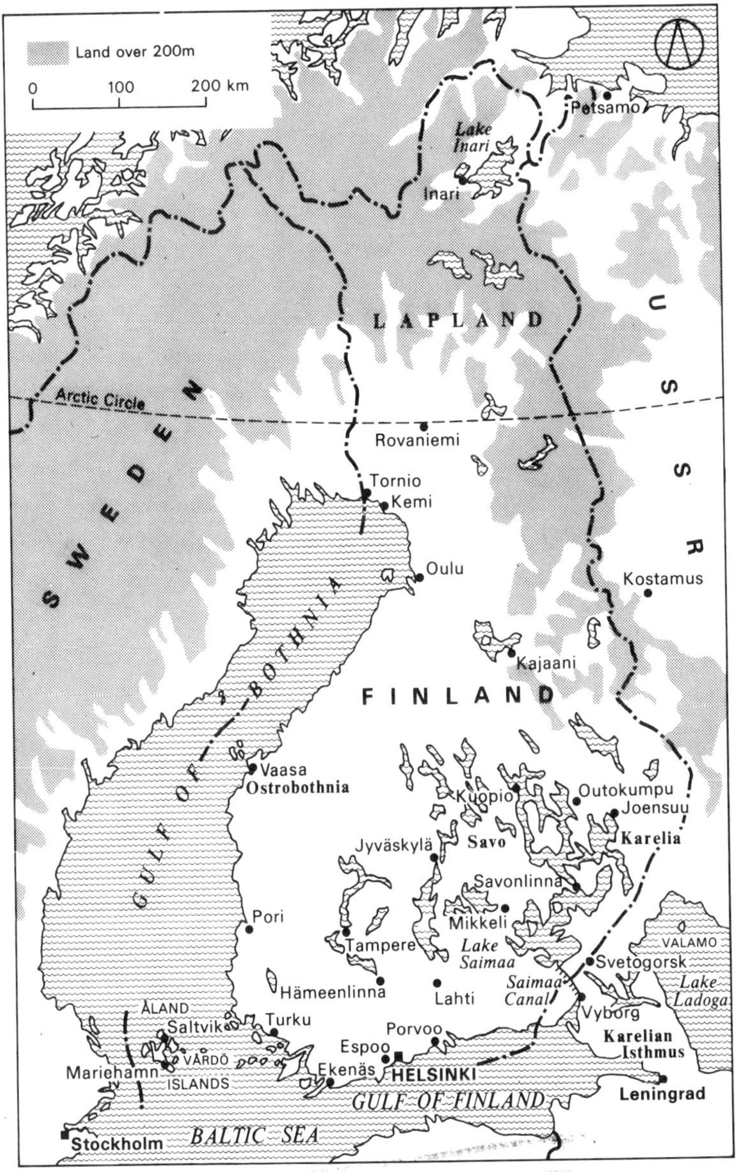